This collection of recipes and stories was inspired by years of culinary travels and meetings with wonderful cooks from many different cultures.

Growing up in a rural setting, my own first dishes were wholesome stews concocted from my father's vegetable garden and my mother's spice cupboard.

As a young teenage vegetarian I began a life-long fascination with the huge scope of delicious and nutritious foods: from sweet spiced-packed dhals and powerful raw food salads to the vibrant colours of roast red pepper, beetroot and chocolate chilli and cheeky yellow gnocchi.

Combinations such as these have nurtured my creative cooking skills during the hours spent in my kitchen feeding family, friends, customers and restaurant guests.

This book contains useful tips for the kitchen garden and on both sourcing and conveniently storing cooked wholefoods. It especially emphasises the value of eating natural, fresh and local produce.

Most of these recipes are dairy and gluten free with the option of adding dairy and wheat when desired. They are flavoursome, exotic, easy to cook and fantastic for all age groups.

To dear Laura
with love
Laura Tyler

THE PHOENIX RESTAURANT

Gateway to the Dingle Peninsula

on the R561 between
Castlemaine Village & Inch Beach
County Kerry • Ireland

T: 00353 (0)66 976 6284
www.thephoenixrestaurant.ie

'A Culinary Adventure' by Lorna Tyther
Nominated for Irish Cook Book of the Year.

Editor Lissy Walsh Riechhold

Graphic Design & Photography
Barbara Hodges
M: 00353 (0)87 7431778
E: barbarahodges@eircom.net

A CULINARY ADVENTURE
by LORNA TYTHER

CONTENTS

PULSES • GRAINS • TOFU	2 - 7
SALADS	8 - 25
SALSA • SAUCES • CHUTNEYS	26 - 41
SOUPS	42 - 51
HEARTY LUNCHES • TAPAS	52 - 75
BAKES • ROASTS • GRILLS • STIR FRYS	76 - 101
STEWS & CHILLI	102 - 107
INDIAN CURRIES & DHALS	108 - 121
SWEETS & DESSERTS	122 - 131

PULSES

All **Beans** benefit from being soaked overnight or at least for a few hours in cold water. If you forget to do this just steep them in boiling water until you need them and add a little longer to the overall cooking time. In both cases change the water before cooking. All beans *(as opposed to lentils)* should be cooked vigorously for 10 minutes without a lid in order to evaporate toxins.

Lentils can be treated similarly, but as they are generally smaller they do not need to be steeped for as long.
With red lentils you get away with washing them in warm water and using directly.

Once you have used a few different types of pulses you will become accustomed to cooking times. Use a double quantity of water to pulses and cook until soft. With green & yellow split peas and chickpeas a frothy scum will appear when the water comes to the boil. Simply skim this off, lower the heat and partially cover, keeping a watchful eye.
If *(per chance)* you are multi-tasking, use a timer.

Soaked pulses begin the sprouting process after a few hours, which is all the better for nutritional value. Once sprouted they need less cooking time and can be perfect for stir frys, soups and falafels. They store well in an airtight container in the fridge for several days by occasionally rinsing & changing the water. Pulses can be used in their whole form in stews, curries or salads. They can be liquidized for purees, such as hummus, or smooth soups; well cooked into a dahl or used as a binding agent for falafels, vegetable burgers & bakes.

Pulses are ideal for combining with whole grains, nuts & seeds or dairy, in order to create all the amino acids needed for a whole protein diet.

Be daring and experimental with pulses; buy a packet you have never seen before, soak them and test the biting quality. If they are very hard, generally they will need plenty of heat and liquid to soften them up.

Try adding some well fried onions, garlic or a carrot for sweetness. The Indian style spices such as cumin, fennel, chilli and cardamon create lovely pungent flavours.

The European herbs like rosemary, thyme, basil and bay, combined with lots of black pepper, create an earthy depth. A generous dash of olive oil, or a knob of butter will enhance taste. Always add salt towards the end of the cooking time, as salt dehydrates and will hinder the re-hydration process of the dried pulses.

The cooled, cooked beans can be kept in the fridge.
If they are in their own cooking liquid and anaerobic they will last about 3 days. They can be drained, tossed in oil and balsamic vinegar for a shelf life of 5-6 days. If they are part of a curry, spicy sauce or a dhal they can easily be kept for up to 4 days.

A useful trick is to freeze cooked, drained beans flat on a baking tray and then break them up in order to store them in bags. This allows you to use the amount you require for your own very healthy fast food.

PULSES

GRAINS

TOFU

3

GENERAL COOKING TIMES:

For soaked pulses:

Butter Beans - 2 hours

Red Kidney Beans and Yellow Split Peas -
1 hour 30 minutes

**Borlotti, Red Aduki, Haricot Beans, Black Turtle Beans
and Split Green Peas** - 1 hour

**Mung Beans; Whole Brown, Black, Green, Beluga
and Puy Lentils** - 45 minutes

Red Lentils - 20 minutes

There are many other types of pulses which can be found
in good Indian stores and wholefood shops.

Dehydration and Rehydration
With any wholefoods there are always slight variables in
regards to the amount of liquid needed for the cooking
process. This is relative to humidity and storage conditions
of the products.

MEASUREMENT:

The measurement of **1 mug** used in these recipes is equal
to the weight of: **8oz - 225gm - 1 American Cup**

GRAINS

In macrobiotic cookery, grains are dry roasted with a little salt
in the cooking pan before water is added. It becomes more
alkaline, *(in macrobiotic terms yang as opposed to ying)*. Add the
water and bring to the boil, reduce the heat, cover and simmer
slowly without stirring. Take a peek and if needed add a dash
more water. Depending on individual taste preferences, as
long as the grains are not hard inside, they are cooked.
At this point turn the heat off, place the pan on a wooden board
and cover with a tea towel. The grain will then swell without
over cooking, allowing the natural flavours to permeate.
Certain recipes may require an *al dente* grain which means it is
firm to the bite when cooked.

Uncooked, soaked pulses or seeds, whole spices & vegetables
may be added to grains. Pulses need ample water and often a
longer cooking time for re-hydration whereas grains absorb
liquid fairly quickly.

The ideal pulse for brown rice would be puy or green lentil,
mung bean or even a well soaked aduki bean. Red lentils
lend themselves better to cooking with millet & quinoa,
still benefitting from being well soaked first.
By combining whole grains with pulses or seeds the protein
value is increased.

Cooked grains can be stored for several days in the fridge,
however it is best to aerate them by lightly lifting them with
a fork pre-refrigeration, making sure they are thoroughly
cooled, as grains hold heat for a long time.

Brown Rice. There are many varieties of wholemeal rice including short and long grain, basmati and red rice. It takes 45 minutes to cook, at a ratio of 2 : 1, water to rice.

Polenta is ground maize which comes in diverse sizes. It cooks differently to other grains therefore I will include a basic method here.

Polenta needs roughly a ratio of 4:1 water to grain respectively. Simmer the salted water with some added stock or herbs, then slowly pour in the polenta whilst vigorously beating with a balloon whisk; it loves to make clumps. Treat polenta with confidence, be firm and respectful, and as soon as it starts to thicken cover it before it sends forth a scorching plop of mixture. Cooking times vary depending on how fine the grain is. Finely ground polenta should cook in 5 minutes; medium ground in 10 minutes, and coarse ground maize will take 20-30 minutes.

Buckwheat is a nutty, alternative grain which is greatly improved by dry roasting until the grain slightly darkens; after which, cooking time is about 10 minutes.

Barley has a great springy bite. Treat like brown rice. It is not only useful for soups but it also gives a great texture to burgers and bakes. Cooking time is about 45 minutes.

Millet is a grain that is high in calcium. It is cooked by first dry roasting and then adding a ratio of 2:1 water to grain. Cooked millet holds together well and is good for burgers and pasties. Cooking time is 20 minutes.

Quinoa

A member of the amaranth family, quinoa is a seed and a complete protein. It can be soaked and eaten raw rather like bulgur. When cooking it can be treated in a similar way to millet; it is, in fact, lovely when mixed with millet and makes a very nutritious bake.

Quinoa flakes are a useful substitute for breadcrumbs and can be added in baking to replace wheat flour.

All the grains can be dressed up or down; made bland or spicy. They all make a perfect meal in a pot, like a risotto, paella, stir fry or a pilau.

Bulgur is a coarsely cracked wheat which can be cooked for a maximum of 10 minutes and eaten hot or soaked in cold water and used for a taboule salad.

Kamut and **Spelt Wheat** are ancient strains of wheat. They **may** be suitable for people with wheat intolerances.

Tamari is a soya based condiment similar to soya sauce but is wheat and sugar free. It gives steamed grains a wonderful flavour and increases their protein value.

Flours

Most of the gluten free grains, are available as flour or flakes. We are accustomed to corn flour which is finely ground maize. Chick pea or Gram flour is used for desserts in India and Napal. When buying alternative flours, the only thing to remember is... to be experimental and use them.

My mother has replaced wheat for organic brown rice flour, in her age old traditional crumble recipe, and she loves it !

TOFU

Tofu is a protein source, originating in the Far East and made from soya beans.

First the beans are processed to extract a milky substance; then they are curdled, and the solids separated by straining, in a method not unlike the first stages of cheese making. The soya curd is produced within a day and can be used immediately or pressed for a few days to form a drier, firmer tofu. It is a malleable and versatile substance which may be used as a dairy substitute, or even, texture-wise, as a meat replacement. In recent years it is produced in most European countries and can even be made in a domestic kitchen.

There are 2 main types of tofu.
The first one, **Silken Tofu**, is soft and better for creaming into toppings, desserts or smooth dips.
Then there is the **Solid** or **Firm Tofu** which can be bought flavoured or plain. These cut well into cubes, flat slices or strips and can be seasoned or soaked in a marinade before being fried or steamed. They can be used as part of another dish or served separately, simply as a tofu steak.

Tempeh is a soya curd made with the whole fermented bean, which gives it a stronger taste.
It can be sourced in Health Shops, Asian Grocers and places like the English Market in County Cork.

Tofu is often on the menu in Chinese, Thai or Japanese restaurants. Commonly it is deep fried and served with cashew nuts. It may be used in seaweed wraps for its springy consistency and pure whiteness which contrasts well with other ingredients.

When tofu is cooked it swells slightly and seals, and if fried it will form a slightly crispy surface. It absorbs the flavours and colours of the ingredients it is cooked with. It lends itself well to traditional far eastern flavourings such as soya sauce or tamari and goes very well with sesame seeds, toasted sesame oil, lemon, garlic and spicy curry pastes.

When raw it can be liquidized with oils and lemon to work as an emulsifier and as an egg replacement in mayonnaise or creamy desserts.

Tofu is naturally low in calories and is easier to digest than beans as it has, like yoghurt, undergone that first stage of digestion.

It keeps well in the fridge, becoming firmer and stronger in flavour the longer it is kept.

Tofu is usually sold vacuum packed in its own whey which is discarded before cooking.
You will find tofu in any good wholefood shop and some supermarkets, in the refrigerated section.

Autumnal Abundance & Trudi's Cucumber Salad

I went to live in Switzerland when I was still a teenager and to begin with it felt transient. Then, I fell in love, married, learnt the language, and by the age of twenty began having babies. These days it just would not do; twenty year olds are finishing degrees, embarking on careers and are often still being home reared.

My mother-in-law, Trudi, was a city dweller but she originated from a farming background. Her native homestead was a small-holding in Bern and we often visited to help out with the autumn harvests.

I learnt then, how close to the earth Swiss farmers are. The farm produced a huge variety of fruit and vegetables, taking to market anything from, freshly gathered wild mushrooms, sweet chestnuts & walnuts, to dried fat runner beans carefully threaded onto cotton strings; along with bunches of beet, root vegetables, winter cabbages & salads, including the last of the summer tomatoes, cucumbers & squashes. There were apples of all descriptions and rich flower bouquets cascading with the deep crimson or creamy white of the poignantly named 'Love Lies Bleeding'. There were also fascinatingly pretty straw flowers, bright copper & purple daisies and transparent feathery grasses, Chinese Lanterns, fragile sprigs of opaque Honesty and seed laden giant poppy heads.

When Trudi and I returned to her modest flat in Zurich, we were richly laden with harvest fare, which was carefully stored in her pristine cellar.

During the following months I would receive wrinkled, but oh so tasty apples, dry earthy potatoes, beet, cabbages, and coarse leaved winter lettuces.

The cucumbers which were grown on the farm were fat and prickly, often bitter with over-ripe seeds and tough with yellowed autumnal skins. However, this was no deterrent to a frugal Swiss 'house frau'.

Every Friday I headed for Trudi's with my baby daughter, Amy, tucked warm in her baby sling. Traditionally a meat free day in Swiss cuisine, my bizarre vegetarianism met sweetly with old school tradition and I learnt many a tasty dish on this day of abstinence.

SALADS

As this is my mother-in-law's recipe, I have left the dairy cream and quark in. *(Quark is similar to a more solid type of creme fraiche. It is made from a culture as yoghurt is.)*

As an alternative, place 1 mug of soya cream and the juice of 1 lemon in a blender jug. Whilst blending slowly drizzle in ½ mug of sunflower oil or olive oil. It will emulsify into a creamy non-dairy mayonnaise.

TRUDI'S GLAZED CUCUMBER SALAD

2 Cucumbers
1 teaspoon Salt

For the Dressing:
1 mug Cream
1 mug Quark *or* **Creme Fraiche**
1 Onion, finely chopped
Juice of ½ Lemon
Bunch of fresh Dill, chopped
Pepper
2 tablespoons Olive Oil

Peel, cut lengthways and carefully de-seed the cucumber.
Slice finely, sprinkle with the salt and place in a sieve suspended over a bowl. Press down with a heavy plate and leave for at least 30 minutes.
Whip the cream and fold into the quark.
Add the onion, fresh dill, pepper, olive oil and lemon juice.
When the cucumber turns opaque, squeeze out the excess water in order to distribute and drain off the salt.
Combine all the ingredients to form a lovely creamy salad with a delicately smooth bite.

Serve with steamed potatoes, delicious mountain cheeses and a crisp and colourful mixed salad with red chicory and variegated green winter endive.

10

DEFINE A SALAD

Everyone loves some type of raw food. Children will pick at raw carrots and fruit naturally, and most cooks will take a crunchy bite of the vegetables they are about to use. Even fast foodies eat coleslaw, which, without the mayonnaise is raw cabbage.

The smell of freshly chopped herbs, fruit and vegetables are evocative and enticing to the taste buds.

Raw foods activate vital enzymes in the gut enabling minerals and vitamins to be efficiently extracted. Certain vitamins, such as Vitamin C, are compromised by heat so it is best to include a good selection of fresh, raw food on a daily basis.
Rather than using too many pricey food supplements why not cut the costs and cut the salads !

Salads can be created from vegetables, fruits, seeds and nuts as well as seasonal green leaves.

Dressings can include fruit juices such as: lemon, lime, orange, pomegranate, cranberry or apple. Experiment and create your own fruit vinegars simply by popping some fresh, frozen or dried berries into wine vinegar.

Oils enhance existing flavours as well as creating a lovely smoothness by coating the ingredients. The more expensive, cold pressed oils are strong in flavour and can be used sparingly.

So sharpen your best knife, invest in a handy box grater, and chop around the clock.

Try:

- Grated carrot with lemon and walnut oil, a twist of pepper, some finely chopped apple, chives, sultanas and walnuts.

- Grated raw beetroot with celery and sweet yellow peppers.

- Bulb Fennel with sweet red pepper.

- White chicory and orange.

- Red cabbage, apple and tomato with a touch of fiery chilli peppers.

- White cabbage with toasted hazel nuts and chopped, dried apricots.

- Pineapple and avocado drizzled with lime and sprinkled with cayenne pepper.

- Steamed cauliflower or broccoli florets with coarsely ground walnuts, walnut oil and lightly chopped fresh mustard greens.

- Tomatoes with a finely chopped onion and fresh coriander, drizzled with white balsamic vinegar.

RED CABBAGE SALAD

The technique of marinating the cabbage with lemon and then tossing it in the hot oil, softens it, making it easier to digest.

1 small Red Cabbage, finely chopped
1 mug Sunflower Seed
6 Garlic Cloves, chopped
¼ mug Dried Tomatoes, finely sliced
¼ mug Black Moroccan Olives, chopped
Juice of 1 Lemon
A good dash of Tamari
Black Pepper & Salt
4 tablespoons Sunflower Oil for frying

Place the cabbage in a bowl and mix in the lemon juice and the dried tomatoes.

Shallow fry the garlic cloves until golden and while still sizzling, pour through the cabbage and then add the olives.

Dry roast the sunflower seeds and when they are hot and the colour has deepened, douse with tamari. Toss into the salad with the seasoning.

Serve with plenty of fresh parsley and sliced apple. This salad is designed to be strong in flavour and full of texture. It will keep well for 2 days.

12

GRATED CARROT & ROCKET
with Toasted Pumpkin Seed

Growing rocket is the easiest thing to do; however it gets wild and very strong, especially in autumn. Carrots when grated make a lovely juicy salad and are the ideal sweetener for rocket.

3 medium Carrots
Winter Rocket, a double handful
2 Tangerines *or* 1 Orange, peeled and chopped
1 tablespoon Sultanas, soaked in white wine vinegar
A handful of fresh Grapes, halved
½ mug Pumpkin Seed
½ teaspoon freshly ground Coriander Seed
Juice of 1 lemon
A thumb sized knob of fresh Ginger, grated
Dash of toasted Sesame Oil
¼ teaspoon Salt
Black Pepper

Grate the carrots and sprinkle with the lemon juice.
Stir in the ginger, coriander, citrus fruit, sultanas and the fresh grapes.
Dry roast the pumpkin seed and add to the mixture.
Season and sprinkle with toasted sesame oil.
Lightly tear the rocket, discarding any tough stems and then combine just before serving.

This salad can be served as part of a mixed platter. It looks good next to a white coconut salsa, a taboule salad and a deep crimson beetroot salad. The pumpkin seeds can be substituted with sesame, sunflower, linseed or even some chopped nuts.

If you are making this salad for children chop the sultanas.

CRIMSON BEETROOT SALAD

1 Beetroot, fresh or pre-cooked
2 Beef Tomatoes, skinned & diced
1 Clove of Garlic, crushed
2 tablespoons Balsamic Vinegar
2 tablespoons Honey
A pinch of Salt
Cayenne Pepper to taste

For the Garnish:
¼ mug Sunflower Seed
¼ mug Flax Seed
A pinch of Cumin Seed

If using fresh beetroot, boil it whole for about 1 hour, leaving all the leaves and roots intact. *This will prevent it bleeding and losing flavour.*
Peel while still hot, gently rubbing the skin off under cold running water.

Grate the cooked beetroot using a coarse grater. Add the tomatoes, balsamic vinegar, honey, garlic, salt & cayenne pepper and then toss all the ingredients together.

The Garnish:
Toast the sunflower, cumin and flax seed then lightly grind in a pestle & mortar and sprinkle on top.

Serve with crisp green leaves and baked potatoes.

POK CHOI with Toasted Walnut Dressing

Pok Choi is a type of cabbage with a fairly strong flavour and a great crunch. Lambs Tongue lettuce is a winter luxury and is full of iron. Using roasted, crushed walnuts in a dressing is so easy and turns any basic salad into something exotic. These flavours all meet head on and compliment each other.

1 small Pok Choi head, chopped
1 bowl of Lambs Tongue Lettuce, well washed
1 Leek, sliced into fine rings
3 Carrots
Juice of 1 Lemon
1 Pear, finely chopped
5 Dried Apricots, chopped

For the dressing:
100 grams Walnuts, chopped
2 Garlic Cloves, finely diced
1 tablespoon Honey
¼ mug Olive Oil
¼ mug Balsamic Vinegar

Dry roast the walnuts in a frying pan, lightly pressing them with the back of a wooden spoon to break them up a little more. Add the olive oil and the garlic and lightly sauté - don't over heat. Blend in a spoonful of honey and then add the balsamic vinegar. Set aside.

Put the lemon juice in a bowl and grate in the carrots, mixing them well to stop discoloration. Add the pear, apricots, pok choi and leek along with the dressing. Just before serving, toss in the lamb's tongue lettuce.

This salad makes a great lunch served with some steamed rice and creamy raita.

NUTTY POTATO SALAD

Potatoes are a wonderful ingredient for a salad, either with a creamy mayonnaise sauce or a simple oil and lemon dressing. The celery and cashews give a little bite and the apples a touch of sweetness.

4 Waxy Potatoes, peeled
2-3 Celery Sticks
2 Apples, peeled
1 dozen or so Green Olives
1 mug Cashew Nuts, lightly chopped
Juice of 1 Lemon
½ mug of hot Vegetable Bouillon
Fresh Parsley, Thyme and Oregano, chopped
Salt & Pepper to taste
¼ mug of Olive Oil

Dice the potatoes into bite sized pieces, place over a steamer and cook until barely soft. Remove from the heat and run quickly under cold water in order to stop the cooking process.
Place the cooked potatoes in a bowl with the hot vegetable bouillon and allow it to soak in. Dice the celery and apple into the lemon juice to stop it discolouring.

Dry roast the cashew nuts, then gently mix all the ingredients together with the olive oil, adjusting the seasoning to taste.

Alternatively, to create a creamier effect, add a home-made mayonnaise instead of the olive oil.

This salad keeps well in the fridge and is useful for a dinner party as it can be made in advance. Potato salads are used in Spain as tapas and are served on little squares of toast topped with finely sliced green onion or marinated red peppers.

SIMPLE MUNG BEAN SALAD

Most of the smaller pulses are ideal as side dishes to serve with anything from a curry to an accompaniment for other salads. Mung beans, aduki beans, puy lentils and green lentils are fantastic as they can all be cooked slightly *al dente*, creating texture. It is important to emphasise how useful it is to cook extra pulses, and pop some in the fridge or freezer for later use. This salad shows the simplicity of a few basic ingredients.

2 mugs lightly cooked Mung Beans

For the Dressing:
¼ mug Oil
¼ mug of Balsamic Vinegar
Juice of 1 Lemon
2 tablespoons Honey
**A handful of Fresh Parsley, finely chopped, plus
    a generous twist of Black Pepper**
¼ teaspoon Salt
¼ teaspoon Madras Curry Powder

For the Garnish:
1 small Onion, very thinly sliced
Sprouted Cress or Alfalfa

Toss the warm mung beans into the dressing.
Serve warm topped with the garnish.

Anything can be added to the dressing, from a good squeeze of tomato paste, a generous spoonful of pesto; to that fast food trick, a spoonful of your favorite curry paste.
This makes tasty tapas and keeps for several days in the fridge.

17

WARM MILLET SALAD

Salsify are available in winter. They are long black roots that when peeled are stark white. They are best steamed and cold shocked in order to retain their crisp, nutty texture and flavour.
Although sticky to peel they are well worth the effort and are, by reputation, an aphrodisiac.

1 mug Millet
1 mug Puy Lentils pre-soaked in 2 mugs of Water
2 mugs Water
1 teaspoon Turmeric Powder
1 teaspoon Cumin Seed
1 teaspoon Tamarind Paste
4 Salsify Roots
1 small colander of French Beans, topped and tailed
10 Cherry Tomatoes
¼ teaspoon Salt

For the Dressing:
4 Garlic Cloves, diced
100 grams Pine Nuts
1 tablespoon Raisins, chopped
Juice of 1 Lemon
Handful of garden fresh Mixed Herbs, chopped
½ teaspoon Salt
Black Pepper
4 tablespoons Pumpkin Seed Oil
Sunflower Oil for frying

Dry roast the millet with the salt; add the water, puy lentils, turmeric and cumin. Stir the tamarind in well and simmer until the grain is *al dente*, for about 20 minutes. Towards the end of the cooking time, add the whole tomatoes and then set aside.

Meanwhile, peel the black roots in a large bowl of water as this prevents them becoming too sticky. Chop them into 1 inch long chunks.
Cook in a steamer for about 5 minutes then add the French beans.

When the vegetables are just cooked, cold shock them under running water and set aside.

Gently fry the pine nuts, raisins, pepper and garlic in the oil.

Fluff up the millet, squeeze in the lemon juice, oil, herbs and salt.

Carefully combine all the ingredients, making sure the millet is well coated with the dressing.

Serve with sweet chutney and drizzle with a spicy balsamic dip.

18

In the Beginning... once upon a time...

My partner Pierre and I were working on a health farm in Dudingen, Switzerland, when I thought I could be pregnant. I was strong, fearless and at 10 I felt worldly, womanly and all knowing; more so than I do now, if truth were known.

Part of the farm house was used by an esoteric group of vegan, raw foodists, who followed what was probably one of the first movements in 'Positive Thinking'. They were alarmingly vociferous chanting "Ich bin – I am", whilst vigorously pacing in front of mirrors and staring wild eyed at their reflection. The wood built house shook to its shallow foundations, consequently my pregnancy test proved negative.

I put my thickening waist down to increased muscles caused by pushing wheel barrows of sand up the hillside, my enormous appetite due to the expenditure of energy hauling the same wheelbarrow and the odd tantrum and tears down to the fact I lived with deranged people, As my previously buoyant breasts tingled in a world all of their own and grew, inevitably succumbing to the earths pull; I merely felt "grown-up" and that it was about time to don a bra.

We decided to get married. and I registered in Hönng, Zurich, where we had previously been living in a large commune with friends. I was granted three months residency on my tourist visa – time enough to organise a wedding. I scoured the sumptuous second hand shops and found a perfect pair of brick-red brocade curtains, out of which our tailor friend, Joe, created a queenly medieval gown.

Meanwhile back at the farm our work continued...
There was already an abundant supply of salads and herbs growing in hot beds and sheltered areas in the garden and I munched my way through succulent bowls of greenery daily. Breakfast was muesli brimming with fresh fruit. My mid-morning snack was fusion food; a lovely lentil & vegetable dhal topped with real Parmesan and heaps of black pepper.
For lunch and dinner, great steaming plates of wholemeal vegetable rice or millet and young beetroot & spinach salads slathered in tahini dressing. Hard work encourages a healthy appetite. I made cinnamon spiced cakes and flapjacks rich with dried fruit & nuts in the massive out-door solid fuel oven.
I grazed on sweet carrots; baby fennel & crisp kohlrabi pulled fresh from the garden, washed clean in the nearby lake.
Preoccupied with hunting & gathering, I spotted a herd of goats on the mountain side. I was given permission to milk them by the curious farmers who laughed, gruffly informing Pierre "If she could even catch them, let alone milk them, *wilcommen*"! Ravenously inspired, of course I could and once tethered they were surprisingly docile. I made yogurt, kefir to drink and a soft cheese which I strained through a muslin cloth on an upturned stool and then rolled in tender chives & cracked black pepper. This delicacy was devoured with great chunks of bread; olive oil oozing down my chin as I smacked my lips with gusto.

We returned to the villa in Zurich a few days before our big wedding date. Our friends began baking and preparing for the party. Pierre organised his old band of gypsy musicians for the day and we were all set.

On the eve before the wedding my girlfriends asked me if I was really sure that I was not pregnant. They marched me down to the local pharmacy for a new test which of course - was positive.

The wedding day was sparkling with June warmth. Happily my dress was only a little tight around the bust and as camouflage we stuffed an enormous, blooming red rose, deep into my bulging cleavage. The city hall was splendidly stately, as I was too, in my flowing vintage robe. It was a beautiful ceremony, with the German translated precisely and with feeling into English. The moment I will always remember, is the awe in the registrar's eyes as I bent over to sign my vows and the weight of my breasts forced the rose to pop out and bounce, blood red, over the solemn desk.

Laughing at the sheer fun of it all, we left the cool, sombre building. Outside, bright shards of light reflected off the Lake of Zurich, catching the effervescent bubbles from our champagne and then I felt the magic & joy that all this time, inside of me, I had been feeding my very own, newly formed precious baby. It all made sense and on top of everything - I was starving!

21

RAW RED HUMMUS

Sprouting is a wonderful way to squeeze every bit of nutrition out of seeds, grains or pulses. All you need is water to create a valuable and relatively cheap power food. Soak them overnight, wash daily and keep covered in a cool spot for use every day in salads, soups & stews or stir-fry's.

They will continue to grow happily for about a week. Refrigeration will slow down the sprouting process and keep them longer. The trick to sprouting small seeds such as alfalfa or cress is regular, gentle watering.

4 mugs Sprouted Chick Peas, washed
A dash of water, as needed
Juice of 2 Lemons
2 - 4 Cloves of Garlic
½ mug Olive Oil
2 medium Raw Beetroot, freshly grated
2 juicy Pears, cored and peeled
Sprig of Parsley
2 tablespoons Tahini
A twist of Pepper & Salt to taste

Place the liquid ingredients and the garlic into a blender and blend well.

Add the chick peas, beetroot, pears & seasoning and blend until really smooth, you may need a dash of water, depending on the liquid content of the sprouts. Finally add the tahini.

This is going to be pink & potent. Sometimes I add a fat, fresh red chilli to the blend for a fiery touch.

Now slice up bright orange carrot sticks, some long crunchy celery put your feet up and press PLAY.

SPROUTED MUNG BEAN RISSOLES

2 mugs sprouted Mung Beans, washed
4 tablespoons Olive Oil
Juice of 1 Lime
½ teaspoon Peri-Peri
½ teaspoon Salt
A dash of Water, as needed
1 large Onion, finely chopped
5 - 6 large leaves of Perpetual Spinach *or*
    young Chard, finely chopped
Fresh Ginger, *golf ball size*, finely chopped

Blend the bean sprouts, oil, lime & spices, the
mixture needs to have a firm juicy consistency.
Add a little water if needed. Stir in the onion,
spinach & ginger and mix well. Using two dessert
spoons form small balls and shallow fry,
flattening them slightly with the spatula before
turning. They will need 2-3 minutes each side.

Alternatively place the rissoles onto a baking tray or into
cup-cake forms and bake in a medium hot oven for 20 minutes.

This mixture also works well as a tasty raw spread or as a filling
for stuffed vegetables such as field mushrooms, aubergines &
tomatoes. All the blended sprout mixtures can easily be rolled in
cabbage, chard or vine leaves, covered with foil and then baked.
Experiment with other types of sprouted pulses such as
aduki beans or diverse lentils for these tasty nutritional snacks.
Store the uncooked mixture in the fridge for 2-3 days.
The cooked rissoles keep at least 5 days refridgerated.

TEN A DAY

This is our Phoenix power food which we sell so well every market day. Everyone loves it, as it is sweet, fresh and crunchy... bursting with flavour and pure energy.

Juice of 2 Lemons & 1 Lime
3 4 Carrots
2 Sticks of Celery
2 Eating Apples, cored
2 Pears, cored & peeled
1 Fennel Bulb
3 Red & Yellow Peppers
1 Orange, peeled
1 mug sprouted Mung Beans
2 mugs Brown Rice, cooked and cooled
1 mug Sunflower & Pumpkin Seeds, toasted in Tamari
1 large colander of seasonal Fresh Herbs, chopped

For the Dressing:
1 large thumb sized knob of Ginger, grated
¼ mug Olive Oil
¼ mug Tamari
A good twist of Black Pepper

Squeeze the lemon and lime into a large bowl then coarsely grate in the carrots.

With your sharpest knife, finely chop all the rest of the fruit and vegetables, add them to the bowl and stir well to prevent discolouration.

Mix in the rice, bean sprouts, the dressing and top with fresh herbs and the toasted seeds.

Serve alone, on a bed of fresh leaves or as part of a tapas plate; it is perfect too, lightly steamed.

It keeps for a few days in the fridge, although as the days go by it will soften as the dressing works on the fruit and vegetables.

We also add other ingredients such as pineapple, grapes, mustard greens, cucumber, baby spinach, leeks, beetroot, and whatever is ripe and available. We avoid using onions, tomatoes, cabbage, garlic or vinegar and advise eating the salad on the day of purchase for optimal goodness.

Sweet Chilli Sauce & Sweeter Revenge

There are many ways to turn that fiery queen of spices, the chilli, into a delicious tongue tingling or sometimes, a tortuous experience.

As a child we were exposed to exotic foods by a bold culinary mother and a father who seemed to delight in inviting weird and wonderful people to our home; often testing mum's patience, imagination and household purse strings.

Although food always seemed abundant in our house, in retrospect, I realize this was due to my mother's expert ability to utilize her store cupboard's last crumbs and create a feast out of nothing.

One day, a hungry assortment of adults and kids returned from the judo club which my father ran in the local school. Dad, rather high in spirits, demanded spicy cheese sandwiches to be prepared immediately by his good wife.

Diligently mum scurried to the kitchen and in her usual form she returned laden with delightful mouth watering titbits. His, was on a special plate and was respectfully presented to Him first. Seconds later dad was spluttering, choking, popeyed and startlingly purple.

No, it wasn't arsenic, just a well concealed jalapeno chilli. Quietly handing my father a glass of water to soothe the heat of his well swallowed pride, mum smiled the smile of a woman so very perfectly in control of her domain.

Just in case...

Take 5 or more dried chilli pods, a handful of garlic, and fry them in olive oil until the garlic is just past golden and the chilli has turned a deep red.

Remove from the heat, add a slice of organic lemon and the juice of the same; add a few over-ripe, fresh tomatoes or a tin of quality tomatoes.

Pour in a healthy dash of tamari, a cup of balsamic vinegar and two chopped apples.

Simmer with a teaspoon of salt, and, when everything is soft; remove from the heat and allow to cool.

For that extra zingy mouth watering taste add a handful of fresh coriander, and then liquidize well.

Serve with fajitas on a sandwich, or use as a dip for any thing... and, if your partner is playing up simply use your imagination.

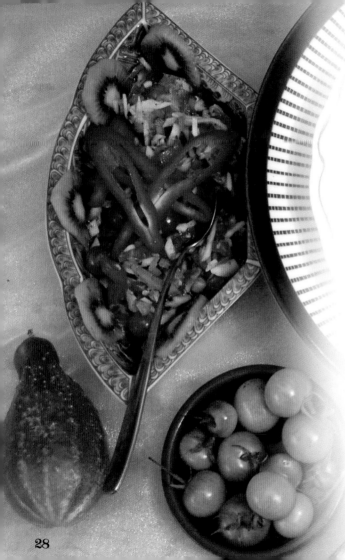

FRUIT SALSA

Salsa is the Spanish word for sauce. In countries as warm as Spain or Mexico, with their abundance of fresh fruit and vegetables, it generally implies a cold sauce usually made with finely diced raw ingredients.

Here in the cooler climes we too can make salsa and use anything that gives a tangy sweetness; usually with a hint of spice such as chilli.

One thing that is needed for a salsa is a very sharp knife. Purchase a good one, learn how to sharpen it, and guard it well.

Here is an example of a kiwi salsa, as an alternative to using tomatoes.

4 Kiwi Fruit, peeled and diced
1 Onion, finely diced
1 Eating Apple, peeled and diced
A generous sprig of Coriander & Parsley, chopped
A thumb sized knob of fresh Ginger, diced
1 small fresh Chilli Pepper, diced
Juice and zest of 1 Lime
Salt & Pepper

Place all the diced ingredients onto a large chopping board, sprinkle the mixture with some salt and give it an extra good chop.

Sweep everything into a bowl and season to taste.

Serve the same day with any of the Bean Chilli recipes.

DEEP CRIMSON SALSA

This winter salsa combines solid earthy tastes with zesty fruit. The addition of the sweetcorn creates both texture & colour and the fresh thyme leaves a lingering aroma of hot summer days.
Of course, this can be made in summer with early beetroot, in which case they could be added raw, finely chopped, or grated.
Cooked organic beetroot is often available in handy vacuum packs.

4 small Beetroot, cooked & diced
1 Green Apple, peeled & diced
1 Pear, peeled & diced
4 Tomatoes, diced
¼ Red Cabbage, finely diced
2 Corn Cobs *or* 1 tin Sweet Corn

For the Dressing:
Juice of 2 Lemons
Small bunch of fresh Thyme, finely chopped
2 Garlic Cloves, finely diced
2 tablespoons White Balsamic Vinegar
Salt and Pepper
2 tablespoons Olive Oil

Cook and remove the corn from the cob.
Combine all the fruit & vegetables and coat generously with the dressing.

Serve with some creamy hummus and crunchy cos lettuce. This salsa keeps well refridgerated.

PESTO

Pesto is always unique to the region, the season and to the person making it. Only recently I was told of a recipe which included creamed potato along with the classic Pine Nuts, Basil, Olive Oil and Parmesan. Definitely worth trying. Here is our nut and dairy free version.

1 large colander of Garden Fresh Herbs, washed and drained
4 heads of Garlic, peeled
½ mug organic Lemon Juice
Juice of 2 fresh Lemons
½ mug Olive Oil
½ mug Sunflower Oil
2 teaspoons Salt
2 mugs organic Sunflower Seed
1 teaspoon Peri–Peri
A good twist of Black Pepper

Place the garlic, oils, lemon juice and seasoning into a blender jug and blend until really smooth.

Lightly chop the herbs and add to the mixture along with the sunflower seeds and blend again.

Depending on the time of the year and the type of herbs, you may need to add a little more oil and lemon.
In summer and early autumn we have plenty of basil.
In spring we use lots of chives, oregano, sage and fennel.
Parsley seems to be abundant every season!

To store pesto, cover well with olive oil and keep in an airtight container in the fridge for up to 3 weeks.

HERB OIL

For diverse herb oils use less garlic, omit the sunflower seeds and add more oil. Try fresh floral combinations such as: rocket with chive flowers or dill with thyme flowers.

AIOLI *(a creamy mixture of garlic and oil)*

Blend garlic, lemon, sunflower oil & salt and slowly drizzle in olive oil to form a rich and creamy emulsification.

Herbs have a natural rise and fall of sap during the day, eleven in the morning is the optimal time to harvest succulently scented herbs.

PERI-PERI is a Portugese mixed spice consisting of dried chopped chilli and herbs.

SWEET RED PEPPER SALSA

This is such a simple cooked salsa, which can also
be used to stir through pureed pulses, such as
creamed butter beans or mashed turtle beans.
It is lovely tossed through steamed sweet potatoes
and it can tart up a humble potato salad into a
mouth watering delight.
Let your imagination run riot.

3 Onions, very finely diced
3 Red Peppers, finely diced
1-2 fresh Red Chilli Peppers, finely diced
Juice of 1 Lemon
2 teaspoons Sweet Paprika
¼ teaspoon Salt
2 teaspoons Honey
2 tablespoons Olive Oil
Sunflower Oil for frying

Gently fry the onion, peppers and chillies in the
sunflower oil. Add the lemon juice, paprika, salt
and a dash of water.
Slowly simmer until all ingredients are soft.
Stir in the olive oil and honey.

Serve as a condiment to butternut squash steaks,
a frittata, as a tapas; or simply spread thickly on
my husband Billy's freshly baked bread.
It keeps for about 5 days in the fridge
(if it ever gets there) !

FRESH CHUTNEY

Most Indian meals will include fresh chutney and a fruity or even creamy salad aimed to refresh the palette in between the heavier, stronger flavours of curries and dahls.

Thanks to ancient and prosperous spice routes which gave birth to global fusion cuisine, we can nearly always find just the thing we need for an exotic and unusual chutney in our fruit bowl, vegetable box or larder.

So look for something crisp, sweet or smooth *(mango, papaya and coconut spring to mind)*, combine it with a hint of spice, fresh coriander, a drizzle of lime and serve in small portions, one tablespoon per person.

Crisp:
Matchstick chop a carrot, sprinkle with lemon and season. *Too simple?*
Then add a generous handful of mint, and a finely chopped yellow or red pepper. Top with a few toasted sesame seeds.

Spicy:
Long white radishes are very popular in India. Coarsely grate them with some lightly toasted black mustard seeds, pepper, salt, lemon and chilli.

Sweet & Fruity:
A mixture of fresh and dried fruit such as dates, avocado and ripe pears, finely chopped with plenty of black pepper, fresh ginger, a sprinkle of salt and a squeeze of lime.

Tart & Creamy:
Pineapple with freshly grated coconut, sweet paprika, a pinch of pepper & salt, drizzled in honey.

Crunchy & Sweet:
An exotic pomegranate, blood red, with finely grated white cabbage, fresh coriander tossed in freshly squeezed orange.

Mellow:
Diced melon topped with cashew nuts roasted in tamari.

Refreshing:
Chopped dried apricots and apple tossed in honey, lime, fresh ginger and poppy seeds.

Adventurous:
- Mashed bananas with chilli oil, lemon and finely chopped tomato.

- Pineapple sliced and sprinkled with peri-peri and chopped pistachio nuts.

- Desiccated coconut lightly fried with spring onions, chopped sultanas, crushed cumin and cardamon seeds.

- Mandarins sliced with mango, sprinkled with with fresh lovage, black pepper, chunky salt and white wine balsamic vinegar.

- Cucumber with chives, toasted sesame oil and fresh ginger.

Swooning? Mouth watering?
Be imaginative by combining everyday ingredients with something unusual and adding a squeeze of citrus.

Remember to use dried fruit, toasted nuts or seeds and if you need a creamy effect use soya cream. Cross continents too, just like our brave culinary pioneers did. If it works it works! You will soon find your own complimentary tastes, textures and colours.

BAKED PUMPKIN & DATE CHUTNEY

This is one of my favorites; it starts with a fussy flurry of roasting and boiling and ends with almost a meal in a jar.

1 mug crushed Dates, chopped
500 grams Pumpkin, cut in chunks
Juice of 1 Lemon
1 mug White Wine Vinegar
¼ teaspoon Salt
2 Chillies, fresh or dried, chopped
Dash of toasted Sesame Oil
2 tablespoons Sunflower Oil
Optional: Soya Cream

Boil the dates with the vinegar and a dash of water.
Sprinkle the pumpkin with the sunflower oil and salt and grill until soft and slightly browned.
Liquidize all the ingredients together.

This makes a smooth chutney or alternatively you can keep half the roasted pumpkin back before liquidizing and add at the end. This way you see the lovely bright yellow pumpkin chunks and have the added texture. The chutney may be mellowed by stirring soya cream in at the very end.

This chutney can be served with a curry, adding a solid sweet spiciness; it is wonderful on toast with some freshly sliced tomatoes and a little fresh coriander. It is delicious tossed through a pasta penne.

COCONUT CHUTNEY

When I was in Sri Lanka there was a real coconut culture in the kitchen. Fixed to every kitchen table is a coconut grinder. The halved coconuts are pressed by one hand onto a spiralled blade while the other hand turns the handle resulting in lovely, juicy, shredded coconut which can be used for any nature of dishes. The Sri Lankans make a gorgeous fresh chutney with coconut, chilli and lime which I used for breakfast, lunch and dinner. On returning home, a coconut junkie, I bought a big bag of desiccated coconut and experimented.

2 mugs Desiccated Coconut
2 Onions, finely chopped
2 Chillies, fresh or dried *(fresh is best)*
½ mug Sultanas, chopped
2 Tomatoes, finely chopped
Juice of 1 Lime or Lemon
¼ teaspoon Salt
2 tablespoons Sunflower Oil for frying

In a frying pan, dry roast the coconut until it becomes a pale golden colour. Add the oil, onion and chillies and fry until the onion is golden. Stir in the sultanas and tomatoes and continue to cook for a few minutes more, finally adding the lemon and salt. This is a dry chutney and can be served as a garnish for curry, a dhal or on any cooked grain. It is also an unusual topping for a crispy salad especially if you serve it as part of a tapas plate. This is the basics of coconut chutney.

Experiment by adding finely chopped pineapple to give a tangier, juicier consistency and a few torn leaves of fresh coriander will add a special zing.

APRICOT & ONION RELISH
with Cardamon

White wine vinegar gives a clarity, both in flavour and colour. Always use a good one.

2 mugs organic, dried Apricots, roughly chopped
2 mugs Water
1 mug White Wine Vinegar
4 Red Apples, diced
2 Red Onions, diced
2 dried Chillies, finely diced
25 Cardamon Pods, husks removed
½ teaspoon Salt
1 tablespoon toasted Sesame Seed Oil
1 tablespoon Pumpkin Seed Oil

Place all the ingredients, except the oils, in a pan. Bring to the boil and then cover and simmer until the apricots are soft, adding more water if it becomes too dry. It should take no more than 15 minutes.

Season, remove from the heat and add the toasted sesame seed oil. To enhance the depth of flavour, add the deep green organic pumpkin seed oil. The oils will give a shiny glow to the relish and will tone down the vinegar.

The relish will keep for about 1 week, mellowing nicely until the last drain is naughtily removed from the jar with the index finger. If it is jarred and sealed whilst roasting hot it will quite happily store for months in its pasteurized state. This sweet and tarty relish is good with potato wedges and especially tasty with sweet potato wedges eaten, feet up, in front of a good film.

SPICED BALSAMIC DIP

I first tasted this dip when lunching with my father in one of his favorite Italian restaurants in New Oxford Street.
We ate it accompanied by some fat and juicy olives and a wonderful bottle of Barolo.

1 mug Red Wine Vinegar
1 mug Balsamic Vinegar
1-2 Chillies, fresh or dried
2 tablespoons Brown Sugar *or* **sugar substitute**
¼ teaspoon Salt

In a frying pan, combine all the ingredients and reduce by simmering very slowly for about 15 minutes.
(The sugar is needed to both thicken & sweeten the dip and substitutes such as: rice or palm sugar can be used.)

The mixture will thicken and become slightly syrupy, if it becomes too thick, a dash of water may be added.
Allow to cool. Use as a drizzle on certain soups or as a tapas dip poured into a white crucible with equal amounts of translucent extra virgin olive oil, served with plenty of bread to dunk. It stores well in an airtight jar.

CUCUMBER & POTATO RAITA

Raita is traditionally made with buffalo yoghurt and cucumber. It should be cool and creamy and will often contain potato, mint or a little saffron. It is served as part of a tali plate, the standard Indian main course, which consists of diverse vegetable curries, at least two dhals, fresh chutneys, popadoms, chapattis, nans and rice.

¾ Cucumber, grated
¼ Cucumber, chopped
½ teaspoon Salt
2 Spring Onions, chopped
1 boiled Potato, diced
1 mug Soya Cream
Juice of 1 Lemon
¼ mug Sunflower Oil

For the Garnish:
A few strands of Saffron *or*
A sprig of Eau de Cologne Mint

Grate ¾ of the cucumber into a sieve, sprinkle with salt and pop a plate on top with a heavy weight, then leave to drain. Meanwhile blend the soya cream with the lemon juice and oil. Place in the fridge to thicken while you chop the spring onion, cooked potato and the last ¼ of the cucumber. Squeeze out the grated cucumber and combine all the ingredients together, season to taste and serve immediately.

Garnish with chopped mint, and for added luxury and gorgeous colour, pound a little saffron with a teaspoon of water and use as sweet aromatic decoration.

37

PHOENIX RICH TOMATO SAUCE

Tomato sauce is as diverse, and often as personal, as the contents of a lady's handbag. It can be anything from a heavily laden ratatouille; to fresh tomatoes warmed through with lightly fried garlic, salt and pepper and then simply topped with a sprig of basil.

Lovely, unique flavours; seasonal, regional and compatible with the accompanying dish.

3 tins Chopped Tomatoes
4 Garlic Cloves, finely chopped
1 dried Chilli Pepper, finely chopped
2 medium Onions, finely chopped
1 medium Carrot, finely chopped
2 sticks Celery, finely chopped
2 Red Peppers, chopped
1 Yellow Pepper, chopped
1 Courgette, chopped
1 Aubergine, chopped
A generous dash of Red or White Wine
Cottage Garden Herbs, ie: Sprigs of oregano, thyme,
    sage, lovage, bay leaves and fresh basil
A good dash of Water
A good dash of Olive Oil
1 teaspoon Salt & Black Pepper to season
2 tablespoons of Sunflower Oil for frying

Heat a large wide saucepan or a good quality wok; add the sunflower oil, garlic and chilli pepper and fry until the garlic just turns golden. Add the onion and sauté until glassy; then add the carrot and celery, followed by the aubergine, peppers and courgette. Let the vegetables soften, then add the tomatoes, wine, water, seasoning and garden herbs.

Lower the heat and simmer for about 50 minutes, stirring occasionally until the vegetables and sauce are one. You may have to add a dash more water.

Remember, reducing infuses flavours by extracting essential oils through sustained heat. Towards the end of the cooking time, add a glug of olive oil, some fresh basil and adjust the seasoning.

This recipe makes a lovely big pot of sauce which keeps for at least 4 days in the fridge and freezes well. When re-heating, start with a dash of water in the pan as it can easily burn.

Phoenix tomato sauce goes well with any pasta dish and most of the bakes, as well as with steamed grains such as wholemeal rice, millet or polenta. To make a spicy tomato sauce *(an Arabiatta)* just pop in an extra chilli pepper or two.

It really is worthwhile finding the best quality tinned tomatoes and most of the organic chopped varieties do have a nice thick juice, surrounding flavorsome chunks of tomato.

AMY'S & STINI'S MIDNIGHT VERSION

When my daughters go out for a night and come back in the small hours, starving, this is what they do:

Finely chop and fry a couple of onions, some garlic and add tinned and fresh tomatoes. Season well with pepper and salt. Reduce the sauce for the time it takes to boil a pan of water and cook some *Al denti* Spaghetti.

Serve with a good twist of pepper, parsley and lots of freshly grated parmesan.

Now that's fresh fast food, at half the price, without the queue or the road rage as the dinner cools on the passenger seat.

The Moon on Castlemaine Harbour

Toasted Flour Sauce

Bechamel Sauce is a classic white sauce. Traditionally it is made by simmering carrot, onion, cloves and a bay leaf in milk and reducing. This is then added to a roux of melted butter and refined wheat flour.

We can substitute the dairy milk with soya, oat or rice milk, use oils instead of butter and gluten free flours such as potato, corn, rice and tapioca flour.

I love to dry roast flour to varying degrees of brownness and add oil, onion and garlic and then proceed from there. A traditional gumbo sauce is made this way, the darker the better. A lightly toasted flour sauce goes well with lightly fried wild mushrooms.

In Switzerland a lovely vegetarian Lenten soup is made during carnival time, whereby the flour is turned to an earthy brown before the onions and stock are added. It is served with crispy garlic croutons and is called Basler Mehl Soup.

I find that a dark roux with a good dash of Tamari, a dollop of rich tomato sauce plus any vegetable stock, makes wonderful gravy.

When I lived in Switzerland I learnt a lot of cooking techniques from a chef who had cooked during his conscription in the Swiss army. Arnoldo kept a little glass of flour and oil next to the cooker to add to any sauce that he felt needed an extra thickener. Believe me, there was never a lump in any sauce that he made:

2 tablespoons of Flour, of your choice
1 Onion, finely diced
½ litre, non dairy Milk
Salt & Pepper
A grate of Nutmeg
2 tablespoons of Olive *or* Sunflower Oil

In a saucepan, dry roast the flour and when golden brown add the oil and the onion. Continue to fry for a few minutes, coating the onion with the flour. Season and add the milk. Keep stirring until the sauce thickens.

Take note of the different ways the diverse flours and non dairy milks behave when used for a sauce. Get to know your products and use what suits you, and the dish, best.

Brown Rice

Potato

Cornflour

Oats

ROUX
SAUCES

Rice Flour
Roux Sauce

Rice Flour
Unroasted

Rice Flour
Roasted

y stepmother makes thick and creamy soups. She simply takes the vegetables my father grows in his garden, then cooks and purees them with a little pepper and salt.

The beauty of these soups lies in the pure flavour of the truly fresh vegetables.

BEETROOT & ORANGE SOUP

Unusual as it is, this soup is loved by all age groups and it is oozing with vitamins.

6 cooked Beetroot, chopped
2 large Sweet Potatoes, chopped
1 Celery stick, chopped
1 thin slice of Orange
Juice of 2 Oranges
4 Garlic Cloves, chopped
1 dried Chilli Pepper
1 teaspoon Cumin Seed
6 mugs of Water
1 teaspoon Salt
4 tablespoons of Sunflower Oil for frying

Lightly fry the garlic cloves, chilli and cumin seed. Add the beetroot, sweet potato, celery and slice of orange. Cover with water and leave to simmer for about 10 minutes. Season, add the orange juice and liquidize well.

Serve with a drizzle of spiced balsamic dip and a sprig of celery leaf.

PARSNIP & APPLE SOUP
with Thyme

This soup combines the earthy and fruity sweetness of parsnip and winter apples. Thyme is always abundant in my garden when all the other herbs have bowed out to the ravages of winter. Its rather bitter floral scent fuses all the flavours well:

3 Parsnips, cut into large chunks
2 Onions, chopped
4 Apples, chopped
A slice of Lemon
Sprig of fresh Thyme
2 mugs Water
2 mugs Sesame _or_ Oat Milk
A grate of Nutmeg
Black Pepper
½ teaspoon Salt
2 tablespoons of
  Sunflower Oil for frying

Fry the onion until glazed, then add the chunks of parsnip. *(At the end of winter, the center of the parsnip may become woody, if so, it will need to be removed.)*

Add the apples, water, milk, lemon, thyme and the seasoning.
Cover, cook until soft and then puree.

Serve with fresh parsley and an extra twist of pepper.

SOUPS

CHARD & TOMATO SOUP

A soup does not always have to be thick and creamy. This soup is great when there is an abundance of chard and ripe tomatoes.

Large colander of Chard, well chopped
2 Yellow Peppers, finely diced
2 Sweet Potatoes, finely diced
10 fresh Tomatoes, peeled and finely diced
5 Garlic Cloves, finely diced
1 teaspoon Coriander Seed, *ground in a pestle and mortar*
A thin slice of Organic Lemon
¼ teaspoon Cayenne Pepper *(optional)*
2 teaspoons Paprika
2 tablespoons Olive Oil
Salt & Black Pepper
4 mugs of Water
Parsley
Sunflower Oil for frying

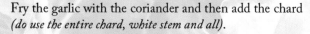

Fry the garlic with the coriander and then add the chard *(do use the entire chard, white stem and all)*.

Add the tomatoes. Pick the ones which are fabulous and sweet today but will definitely be past their sell by date tomorrow.

Add the peppers and potatoes and sauté for a few minutes and then add the rest of the spices.

Add the water along with the lemon slice and simmer until everything is soft.

Remove half the ingredients, including the slice of lemon and liquidize. Return to the pan, season well with salt and pepper and add the olive oil.

Reduce and serve with a sprig of fresh parsley and plenty of black pepper.

Playing with colours

Pre-cooked pulses such as deep red kidney, aduki or even butter beans give a great variation in colour and texture, turning this tangy, light summer soup into a protein rich meal in a bowl.

Instead of serving bread with soup it may be served with a cooked grain such as rice, millet or quinoa. If you have friends or family members who are intolerant to yeast or wheat this can make a pleasant change.

FELI'S & ANNA'S
COLD CUCUMBER SOUP

Every summer we accommodate students and voluntary workers. They come from all corners of the world and are members of WWOOF *(willing workers on organic farms)*.

They are all ages, and learn about cookery, gardening and much more, whilst sharing our work load. I will give an experimental cookery class, which they record, just to see how our excess produce can be utilised in unusual recipes.

One very hot summer we had lots of cucumbers and an abundance of dill. This recipe is what two young helpers, Feli, Anna and I came up with:

6 Cucumbers, peeled, de-seeded, chopped
200 gram pack Silken Tofu
3-4 small Spring Onions, chopped
2 tablespoons White Balsamic Vinegar
Juice of 2 Lemons
1 mug Soya Cream
4 Celery Sticks, chopped
1 bunch of Dill
½ teaspoon Black Pepper
2 teaspoons Salt
1 Chilli Pepper
1 small sprig of Lovage
¼ mug Extra Virgin Olive Oil

Combine all the ingredients, except the olive oil, in an electric blender and process until smooth. Slowly drizzle the olive oil into the mixture while blending. Adjust the seasoning if necessary. Sieve the finished soup and chill it thoroughly.

Dairy cream and home made yoghurt can replace the soya products. Serve with hot toast and olive tapenade.

Lovage is an easy perennial to grow. However it can get very tall and top heavy, so plant it towards the back of your herb garden; it likes a wall. Taste wise it is probably one of the strongest herbs in the garden. In Switzerland its nickname is Magi Kraut because it is the predominant flavouring used in the Magi Instant Soup mixes and bouillon stock cubes. A little goes a long way!

BROCCOLI, FRESH TOMATO & COCONUT SOUP

De-toxing can be fun and it is always challenging to create foods that cleanse the body. The obvious colour in food that purifies is green. Here is a lovely pale green soup to make us beautiful. One of our most common indigenous vegetables is broccoli, which is easy to grow, or to source organically. It can be slightly bitter so we will sweeten it with fresh tomatoes. Coconut is lovely as a luxurious, sweet and creamy thickener.

4 Garlic Cloves
1 teaspoon Coriander Seed, crushed
A colander of Broccoli Florets
2 Carrots, chopped
8 fresh Tomatoes
2 tablespoons White Wine *or* **Lemon Juice**
1 tin Coconut Milk
2 mugs Water
Fresh Parsley, finely chopped
Black Pepper
1 teaspoon Sunflower Oil for frying

For the Garnish:
Baby Vine Tomatoes, intact, vine and all
1 teaspoon Olive Oil
1 teaspoon Balsamic Vinegar

Lightly fry the garlic cloves with the coriander seeds. Add the broccoli, carrots and fresh tomatoes. Add the water with the white wine or lemon juice. Allow to simmer until soft and then liquidize with the coconut. Season with pepper and fresh parsley. For the tasty and structural garnish, sprinkle the baby tomatoes with oil and vinegar, grill, and then simply rest on top of the soup.

JERUSALEM ARTICHOKE SOUP

Jerusalem artichokes are the knobby tubers of a tall plant which has small yellow flowers; it resembles a weedy sunflower. It is perennial, dying down in winter and re-growing every spring. Left without harvesting the tubers will become smaller and increasingly difficult to prepare. Therefore, if grown as a food, they are best dug up and a row of strong ones re-planted each year.

500 grams Jerusalem Artichoke Roots
2 large Onions, chopped
2 sticks of Celery, chopped
3-4 Bay Leaves
1 carton *(200ml)* **Soya Cream**
1 teaspoon of Walnut Oil *(optional)*
2 mugs Soya Milk
2 mugs Water
½ teaspoon Fenugreek Powder
Salt & Pepper
Sunflower Oil for frying

Scrub the artichoke roots with a vegetable brush *(It will be necessary to cut them a little in order to clean them properly)*. Gently fry the onions in sunflower oil with the celery and Fenugreek. Add the artichokes and slowly sauté with a lid on for 15 minutes, then cover in the water, milk and cream; add a few bay leaves and allow to simmer until soft. Remove the bay leaves, liquidize and season.

This soup has a very deep nutty taste and goes well with a drizzle of walnut oil and plenty of black pepper.

COURGETTE & LEMON SOUP

In August we, and everyone we know, become over-run with a growth explosion of courgettes. If the courgettes are really large with tough skins they will need de-seeding and peeling. Here is a very simple summer soup which is thick yet incredibly smooth, light and refreshing.

1 large colander of Courgettes, roughly chopped
2 Potatoes, chopped
3 large Onions with the green stems, chopped
Sprig of Lemon Thyme
A small bunch of Lemon Balm
Zest of 1 Lemon
Juice of 2 Lemons
1 teaspoon Yellow Mustard Seed
4-6 mugs Water, *depending on water content of courgettes*
Salt & Pepper
¼ mug Olive Oil for frying

Put some olive oil in a pan and slowly sauté the onions. Add the thyme, mustard seed, potato and the lemon zest with the courgettes.

Cover with water and simmer until the vegetables are soft.

Season with salt and pepper, the lemon juice and the leaves of the lemon balm and liquidize until everything is totally smooth.

Serve this elegant, lemon tinged soup with a swirl of soya cream or fresh cream and a sprig of thyme.

RED PEPPER, CARROT & LENTIL SOUP

A tasty classic. If there is anything I always have in my store cupboard, it has to be red lentils and carrots.

2 mugs Red Lentils, soaked
2 Onions, chopped
500 grams of Carrot, chopped
3 Red Peppers
3 Apples, chopped
Juice of 1 Orange
4 mugs Water
1 mug of Non-Dairy Milk
1-2 Red Chillies
2 Star Anise
½ teaspoon of Turmeric
Pepper & Salt
2 tablespoons Sunflower Oil for frying

For the Garnish:
1 mug Orange Juice
1-2 Chillies
2 teaspoons Honey
A sprig of Coriander
A dash of Olive Oil
A peck of Salt

Heat the oil in a large pan. Add the onion and sauté gently until glassy. Add the carrot, pepper, apple, star anise, turmeric and chillies and continue to sauté for a few minutes.
Then add the lentils, orange juice, water and milk, cook slowly for around 30 minutes until soft. Remove the star anise and liquidize until really smooth. Return the star anise to the pan and simmer for a little while, adding salt and black pepper to taste.

This is a sweet, thick soup and so lends itself to a tart garnish. Make a reduction with the garnish ingredients and drizzle it on just before serving.

49

CHARD & GREEN LENTIL SOUP

At The Phoenix we have fresh chard in the greenhouse or garden all year round. It is always asking to be added to everything, and the more we cook it the more it grows, so it's not too hard to do just that.

1 mug Green Lentils, soaked in 4 mugs of Water
Good sized bunch of Chard, washed & roughly chopped
2 Onions, diced
4 Garlic Cloves, finely diced
2 large Field Mushrooms, chopped
2 teaspoons Cumin Seed
2 tablespoons Tamari
2 tablespoons Virgin Olive Oil
Pepper & Salt
Sunflower Oil for frying

Fry the onion, garlic, mushrooms and cumin seed.
When everything is sizzling and the cumin and onion are sending out that fantastic fusion of pungent sweetness, add the chard and lentils.
Simmer for about 30 minutes until soft.
Season to taste and add the tamari and virgin olive oil.

This soup can be completely smooth; or often we will take half out, liquidize, and then add the two versions together.

Serve with a pure white crescent of cream and some freshly chopped chives. This soup is very nourishing and could even be eaten with a portion of wholemeal barley or some chunky potato wedges for a bountiful lunch.

SPLIT GREEN PEA, AUBERGINE, LEEK & MINT SOUP

It is possible to make this soup in winter. Pop a mint tea bag into the soup after pureeing. Remember to remove it!

3 mugs Green Split Peas, soaked in 6 mugs of Water
2 Onions, chopped
2 Garlic Cloves, chopped
2 Aubergines, chopped
2 large Leeks, chopped & well washed
Juice of 1 Lemon
Salt & Pepper
1 large bunch of Mint *(just the leaves)*, crushed
Sunflower Oil for frying

Fry the onion, garlic, aubergine and leek.
Add the green split peas and cook until soft.
This could take as long as 45 minutes and may need a little more water.

Add the mint and the lemon and puree until totally smooth.
Adjust the seasoning.

As a garnish, blend a little soya cream, lemon juice, olive oil and finely crushed mint. Swirl onto the soup just before serving and you will get that beautiful, fresh minty aroma without the mint leaves discolouring.

Pasta Fantasta

nce we had a house in Northern Italy. Every school holiday we would load up our big Toyota bus with kids and friends and head across the Swiss Alps to the Italian border crossing in Brissago. A little further down the road we took the ferry boat which crossed the beautiful Lago Maggiori which, ever so slightly, lessened our journey. We had our first espresso while sailing past the palatial Isola Bella and the resplendent lake side villas, all complete with overflowing flora and exaggerated sculptural architecture. The holiday had begun!

We passed L'ago d' Orta driving through ancient stone villages, many with foundations dating back to the Roman Era. From there we spiralled upwards to the cul-de-sac village of Ameno which rested peacefully on a rich fertile plateau. This would be our home for the summer.

In the evening we could look down across the picturesque lake with its lovely Isola San Giulio lit up and mirrored perfectly in the deep waters. Far into the West, the majestic Monte Rosa was always snow peeked and glowed pink in sultry sunsets. If we waited, the fireflies would sparkle and dance, mesmerising us, until their wicked cousins, the mosquitoes, buzzed and attacked. Sun burnt and weary from long swimming sessions in the lake or secret waterfalls and rock pools, we would rush home to shower, don our glad rags and invade one of the delightful rural restaurants; my beautiful blond bambini the talk of the town.

Each one of these numerous mountain eateries offered specialities well worth repeat visits year after year. Where to start? The *'Battle of' Britain'* made a fabulous *Risotto Con Fungi*, and as it bubbled in the kitchen, even in the overpowering heat of summer evenings, you could smell autumnal crisp days and the deep, damp, earthy flavours of acrid chestnut leaves coolly penetrating your senses.

Pasta dishes were always so very simple. We would travel miles down mountain passes to the grand county town of Novara for the most perfect *Aglio Olio e Peperocini*; a speciality of spaghetti, garlic, olive oil and hot peppers.

There, once, in my culinary ignorance, I asked for parmesan to accompany this dish. The Chef left his kitchen arms waving *"Aspetto non non signora perfavore"*; I received a passionate lecture about flavours and was offered pepper by a sheepishly apologetic waiter, obviously wondering if Chef had diminished his tip.

For this dish the pasta would always be a particularly fine Gage, shiny with oil, *al dente*; proud, erect and bouncy, and served on a roasting plate with the pepper mill hovering. My mouth would be watering and my hands would clutch a restraining glass of Barolo wine in order not to seem too rude by stabbing the bearer of the pepper, in my anxiety to eat.

Castlemaine Harbour

HEARTY LUNCHES · TAPAS

Here goes with the recipe:

For two people: Boil a large pan of water with a teaspoon of salt and add 250 grams of the best quality, thinnest Gage Spaghetti or Fettuccini you can find.

Chunkily chop 8 garlic cloves and 4 small hot peppers. Simmer in a generous dollop of good olive oil until the garlic becomes slightly golden and the peppers turn a deeper shade of orangey red.

Remove from the heat immediately the garlic starts to turn. Drain the very *al dente* pasta and toss briefly in the delicious oily mixture; this latter part should take at the most 3 minutes, as the pasta will still be cooking and absorbing the flavours.

Serve on hot plates to salivating diners, hold the parmesan, bring on the pepper and praise the Lord for the Roman Conquest of culinary Europe.

FALAFELS

Falafels are made with raw sprouted chickpeas and are highly nutritious.

To make falafels you will need to soak the chickpeas for about 24 hours or until they have swelled and just begun the sprouting process. Depending on the air temperature they will soon become crunchy, similar to a raw pea.

2 mugs Chickpeas, soaked & sprouted
2 medium Tomatoes
2 Onions
Juice of 1 Lemon
¼ teaspoon Cayenne Pepper
1 teaspoon Salt
Sunflower Oil for frying   **makes 15-20 falafels**

For the Coating:
1 mug fine Maize Meal
Seasoning, chopped herbs, a touch of Peri-Peri

Rinse the chick peas well and then blend with the tomatoes, lemon juice, seasoning and one of the onions.
When smoothish add the 2nd onion, finely chopped and adjust the seasoning. Rest the mixture for 30 minutes.

Generously cover a large plate with the coating.
Drop a heaped tablespoon of the mixture onto the plate and roll gently to form little balls.
They are quite fragile, so carefully place each falafel onto a plate dusted with the coating and set aside.

Heat a frying pan with a ¼ inch of oil.
Gently drop the falafels into the sizzling oil, patiently waiting for the base to form before turning them over; at this stage you may need a dash more oil. The falafels will only take a few minutes for each side. Drain on tissue.

Serve warm with toasted pitta bread, a tahini or yoghurt dressing & salad; three to four falafels are plenty per person.

They can also be baked in the oven covered in our rich tomato sauce to make a full hearty meal.

An alternative cooking method, which we use a lot for our Farmer's Markets, is to form bigger golf sized balls and then lightly bake them in a medium hot oven for about 20 minutes until they are firm to the touch.
This is then a completely fat free version.

Baked   *Fried*

For an additional creative and nutritious touch add grated raw carrots or other vegetables into the falafel mixture and then fry or bake as above. This is especially nutritious when feeding children.

Raw falafel mix keeps 3 days in the fridge in an air-tight container or they can be pre-formed and frozen.

PANCAKES

Because oats are generally milled alongside other grains such as wheat, they are contaminated with wheat gluten. It is however possible to purchase gluten free oats in most wholefood stores.

Once a year pancakes take precedence over the evening meal. Easy enough to make, with wheat flour and eggs to give flexibility, and milk for consistency. Pancakes, omitting any of the above, need to be a little thicker than traditional ones.

This recipe works well for both sweet and savoury pancakes and they are especially good when stuffed with a filling and baked cannelloni style.

1 mug Rice Flour
1 mug Fine Maize Flour
1 mug Ground Oat Flakes
200 gram pack Silken Tofu *or* any non-dairy Cream
4 mugs Water
2 teaspoons Baking Powder
Squeeze of Lemon
Sunflower or Coconut Oil for frying

Liquidize together the flours, oat flakes, fresh tofu and the water. Add the baking powder, a pinch of salt, a squeeze of lemon and a small dash of oil.
Allow to rest for at least half an hour. At this stage you will know if the mixture needs more water. It should have a creamy consistency; slightly thick but not stodgy.

Heat the frying pan, add a touch of oil, and when hot pour in the mixture. Spread quickly by tipping and rolling the pan. Little bubbles will appear as the base of the pancake seals. Lift gently by sliding a spatula underneath.
They can easily be flipped as long as the base is sealed.

Honey & Lime

Serve with maple syrup, or stuff them with a spinach and mushroom filling, then cover with white sauce and bake.

If potato flour is substituted for oats then the mixture is definitely gluten free.

Savoury Filling with Roux Sauce

57

QUINOA RISOTTO (QUINOTTO)

Fresh forest mushrooms can be sourced in Autumn to replace the dried mushrooms. A good selection of dried mushrooms can be found in food shops all year round.

½ mug Green Lentils, soaked overnight
30 grams dried, mixed Forest Mushrooms, pre-soaked
3 medium Field Mushrooms, sliced
1 mug Quinoa
3 mugs Water
2 Onions, chopped
1 large colander Spinach *or* Chard, chopped
2 sticks of Celery, chopped
1 large Carrot, chopped
1 Red Pepper, chopped
1 glass of White Wine
4 Garlic Cloves, diced
Sprigs of Thyme, Bay Leaves, Oregano
1 teaspoon Salt & a generous twist of Black Pepper
2 tablespoons Olive Oil

Soak the dried mushrooms in warm water. Meanwhile fry the garlic until golden, then add the onion, celery, carrot, pepper and the fresh mushrooms; continue to sauté for about 5 minutes. Add the quinoa and stir in for a few minutes.

Swirl the dried mushrooms around a little, in order to dislodge any grit. Squeeze them out, chop, and add to the quinoa, then carefully add the liquid from the mushrooms *(apart from the last gritty drain)*.
Add the water, lentils, white wine, herbs, salt and pepper.

Cover and cook slowly till the lentils are soft, taking an occasional peek to ensure the mixture is moist and adding a dash of water if needs be. When cooked, drizzle with some olive oil, replace the lid, cover with a tea towel and set aside.

Serve topped with parmesan shavings with a mixed green salad on the side.
It is also fantastic as a filling for roast peppers.

This risotto will keep for several days in the fridge and can easily be transformed into burgers or a bake.

QUINOA FRITTATA

2 mugs lightly cooked Quinoa
½ mug fine Maize Meal
1 mug Water
1 small Celeriac Root, chopped into matchstick pieces
2 Garlic Cloves, finely diced
¼ teaspoon Salt and some Black Pepper
Sunflower Oil for frying

Combine all the ingredients and set aside for a minimum of 30 minutes so the maize can absorb the liquid.

Heat a good heavy bottomed frying pan. Add a nice dash of oil and again, heat well. Pour in roughly 1 inch depth of mixture. After a minute reduce the heat and cover whilst saying a little prayer to the Frittata God.

When the mixture has set, gently prize it away from the sides and base. Using a large plate and a really positive attitude turn the frittata onto the plate. Re-oil the pan, allow to heat up and then slide the frittata back in, cooked-side up and cover. The cooking process will take about 8 minutes per side.

If the frittata sticks to the pan pop the lid back on and rest for 5-10 minutes and then loosen the sides and turn. This frittata can easily be cooked on one side and finished later by heating the uncooked side just before serving

Other root vegetables can be substituted as long as they have a similar cooking time. It is worth experimenting.

Serve hot with some spicy re-fried beans and crisp green leaves.

SWEET POTATO & CREAMY TOFU RÖSTI

2 large Sweet Potatoes, coarsely grated
400 grams Silken Tofu *or* a thick non-dairy Cream
2 Onions, diced
½ mug Water
¼ mug Sesame Seed
1 teaspoon Nigella Seed *(black onion seed)*
1 teaspoon Mustard Seed
1 teaspoon Toasted Sesame Oil
3 tablespoons Sunflower Oil for frying

In a frying pan, dry roast the nigella, mustard and ½ of the sesame seeds until they become hot. Add 1 tablespoon of the sunflower oil, the onion and lightly fry.

Mix *all* the ingredients together in a bowl, apart from the remaining sunflower oil, and stir really well. The potato will be lightly suspended in the creamy silken tofu.

Heat a heavy bottomed frying pan and add ½ the remaining sunflower oil. Using a few sesame seeds gently form 1 inch high rostis and place in the hot pan.
If you happen to have a metal rosti ring, this can be used to form the rosti in the pan as the mixture will be quite soft.

Allow the base to seal and crisp-up and then turn and repeat the cooking process. They will take 3-4 minutes each side.

Serve with a colourful salad or sautéd vegetables.
The un-cooked mixture keeps well for 1-2 days in the fridge.

CRISPY GRILLED CHEEKY YELLOW GNOCCHI

Gnocchi is an Italian classic, a baby dumpling, made with potato, wheat flour and eggs. It is usually baked in a pizza oven and topped with gorgonzola or a tomato sauce.
Here is a cheeky version, simply using polenta instead of the eggs and flour.

1 mug cooked Polenta
2 large cooked Potatoes
2 cooked Sweet Potatoes
Small bunch of fresh Parsley
A good grating of Nutmeg
½ mug Soya Milk
Herb Oil
Salt & Black Pepper
Optional: **Parmesan Cheese**

Cook the polenta according to the basic recipe but keep it fairly dry. Mash all the ingredients together and spread the mixture on a bread board.

When cool cut into bite sized chunks and lightly hand roll forming little balls. Place the chunks into an oiled oven dish. Drizzle with herb oil and grill.
They may be sprinkled with parmesan when you remove them from the oven or simply drizzled with a little herb oil.

Alternatively:
Indent the gnocchi and fill with a dab of pesto or a whole baby tomato. Grill and serve.

STUFFED BAKED POTATOES
with Cauliflower, Olives & Cumin

In our house, baked potatoes can be served as a whole meal laced with butter or hummus and plenty of salt & pepper. Here is an interesting twist which encourages those arch enemies – kids and vegetables – to mix.

Any combinations of vegetables can be used and parmesan can replace the sesame seeds.

4-6 large Potatoes
1 Cauliflower
6 Black Olives, finely chopped
1 teaspoon Cumin Seed
1 teaspoon Sesame Seed
Olive Oil
Salt & Black Pepper

Rub the potatoes with oil and salt and bake in a medium hot oven for about 1 hour.
Chop the cauliflower into bite size florets; add the black olives, the cumin seeds and plenty of seasoning.

Remove the potatoes from the oven and cool slightly. Cut in half lengthways, scoop out the flesh and mix with the vegetables. Firmly stuff the mixture into the potato skins, using the palm of your hands to round the top a little, as you will have a slight excess of filling.

Top with the sesame seeds and re-bake; covering for the first 10 minutes and crisping for the last few minutes. Sesame seeds burn easily so take extra care at the very end.

AELPLER MACARONI

There are a great variety of gluten free pastas available. They are very different from the classic durum wheat and do need to be cooked according to their individual characteristics. Rice pasta lends itself well to this Alpine farmer's dish which traditionally, is rich with cream and an abundance of gruyere cheese. In this recipe soya cream and gomassio replace the dairy.

100 grams Rice Pasta, spirals or penne
3 medium Potatoes, peeled and coarsely chopped
1 mug Water
2 mugs non-dairy Milk
1 Onion, finely diced
3 Garlic Cloves, finely diced
1 Carrot, finely diced
2 small Celery Sticks, finely diced
6 Baby Tomatoes, cut in half
1 mug Soya Cream
½ teaspoon Salt & Pepper
a bunch of Parsley, loosly chopped
½ mug Gomassio
Olive Oil for frying

Fry the onion, garlic, celery and carrot for a few minutes. Add the potato, pasta, and the vegetables, continue to sauté so the flavours are absorbed. Pour in the water and milk, simmer slowly, stirring occasionally.
The cooking time will vary according to the prescribed time on the pasta packet.
If needs be, add a little more water.

When the pasta and the potatoes are *al dente* add the soya cream and the freshly made gomassio *(traditionally at this point, the dairy cream and cheese would be added)*; pop in the tomatoes and the fresh parsley and simmer for just a few minutes more to infuse the flavours.
In Switzerland this dish is always served with cooked apple purée on the side.

GOMASSIO *(A macrobiotic tasty topping)*
In a heavy based frying pan, dry roast ½ mug of sesame seeds with ¼ teaspoon of salt. When the seeds deepen in colour remove from the heat, grind in a pestle & mortar and serve warm.

65

Heavenly Hummus

t eighteen I set off on my world tour; destination India. I had been a vegetarian for a year and was an ardent browser in the Indian grocers. I had already learnt to meditate and loved all things that glittered and glimmered.

In spirit I was already there but would my trusty thumb do the rest! Close your ears daughters of the 21st century. Hitch-hiking had its ups and downs but it was free, and predictably unreliable; no one ever stopped in the rain. It was informative; I could discuss the merits of 'Daf' cabins and 'Merc' engines with the world's toughest truckers.

My geography has always been questionable. I traveled North instead of East and arrived in Copenhagen, Denmark. There I immediately registered for voluntary kitchen work at a Festival of Light, Love & Meditation. Remember, this was the seventies during that post hippie rush for inner peace and enlightenment. Now, a vegetarian who meditates, and is never certain where the next meal is coming from, suffers hunger infinitum; I therefore felt that I had not gone too far off course.

I helped to prepare meals for hundreds with a team of hundreds. We ate big chunky salads made with cabbage, carrots, peanuts, raisins and beans; curries, very similar to the salads but cooked; brown rice that would have rebuilt ground zero and hummus, mixed with a tool that resembled a pneumatic drill. In a word, wholesome.

I had tasted hummus only once before, it being the cheapest dish suitable for a non-meat eater in a Greek restaurant in Hampstead. However it had, since then, remained a culinary mystery and apart from reassuring me it was meat free no one in the restaurant spoke enough English to reveal the ingredients. I did manage to understand that Ken Wood was a very clever chef and from then on he always manifested himself in my food fantasies as a magical, white clad figure, who whisked me to the peeks of gourmeismic paradise.

So it happened that, while everyone else was experiencing blissful Nirvana in Denmark, I was ecstatically licking giant spoons of tahini, peeling barrel loads of garlic and mastering the secret that had staved my hunger in London only months before. Who says prayers are not answered! Hummus has always remained, for me, Nirvana on the taste buds. And did I ever find my Ken? Now that's another story!

TAPAS

HUMMUS WITH A DIFFERENCE

2 mugs cooked Chickpeas
6 Garlic Cloves
Juice of 2 Lemons
¼ mug Olive Oil
2-3 Tomatoes, skinned
3 Spring Onions, chopped
1 tablespoon Tahini
1-2 Chillies
3 teaspoons Paprika
1 teaspoon Salt
A sprig of fresh Coriander

Put the lemon juice, garlic, chillies, oil, herbs, spices and seasoning into a blender and liquidize until all the garlic is smooth.
It should become a thick creamy sauce.
Add the tomatoes and the chickpeas and blend, possibly adding a little of the cooking water from the chickpeas.
When everything is smooth blend in the tahini, check the seasoning and add the spring onions.

Use as a dip or a spread.
It will keep for several days in the fridge.

FUN WITH HUMMUS

● Replace the tomatoes with green stoned olives.
● Add lots of fresh herbs to make a 'garden fresh' herbal hummus.
● Use lots of fresh basil and pinenuts for a lovely creamy, green hummus.
● Fresh ginger, lime and coriander for a hummus with zing!

TAPAS, MEZZE, CANAPÉS and STARTERS
yummy little bursts of flavour...

Creamy dips and spicy salsas to poke with
a carrot stick, to spread on a cracker,
a chapatti, or to smear generously
on a crusty chunk of bread.

Lazily linger over the tapas, lovingly
lick your fingers, at least just enough
so as not to mess up your wine glass.

Smile and laugh with friends and
family, feet up, feet down, standing,
reclined, watching a movie, a sunset,
the boys or the girls... at a wedding,
at a birthday, a christening, and here
it is in black and white... at my funeral
party I want hundreds of tasty tapas!

69

SPICY PEAS PUDDING *please!*

Once a pulse has been cooked it can be used as a standby ingredient to create a variety of dishes. Here is a refreshing paté or spread which can be made with green or yellow split peas. Cooked pulses keep well for several days in an airtight container in the fridge.

2 mugs cooked Split Peas
½ mug Sun Dried Tomatoes, chopped
1 tablespoon Currants, chopped
½ tin Coconut Milk
Big bunch of Flat Leaf Parsley, chopped
Small bunch Rocket Leaves, chopped
Spring Onions, chopped
1 teaspoon Cardamon Seed
1 teaspoon Mustard Seed
2-4 dried *or* fresh Chillies, diced
Juice of ½ Lemon
Sunflower Oil for frying

Dry roast the cardamon and mustard seed. Add oil, the spring onions, dried tomatoes, chillies & currants, and sauté for a few minutes.
Meanwhile mix the parsley & rocket together and combine the leaves with the coconut milk, split peas, lemon and the rest of the ingredients. Adjust the seasoning…
some like it hot so you could add a sprinkle more chillie.

Press into a pudding basin, chill well and serve in slices on toast or as part of a mezze platter with a taboulé salad.

TABOULÉ

Taboulé is a cracked wheat salad from the Middle East.

I fell in love with it in Egypt when I was learning Egyptian
Dance in a hotel which overlooked the Pyramids of Giza.
My soul was fed with the view, my stomach with beautiful
mezze plates and I shimmied like a sphinx on a hot tin roof.
Dum- dum- taka- taka- dum- taka- tak- taka

**2 mugs of washed Bulgur, soaked in vegetable
  stock for 10 minutes**

For the Marinade:
This is a marinade as everything is very finely chopped.
Juice of 2 Lemons
2 Garlic Cloves, finely chopped with a pinch of salt
1 bunch Spring Onions, chopped
10 Tomatoes, skinned and chopped
1 bunch Parsley, chopped
1 bunch Coriander (*only the leaves*), chopped
Salt & Black Pepper
4 tablespoons of Olive Oil

Place all the ingredients into a large mixing bowl, it
will be quite sloppy, and then rest the mixture for at
least 30 minutes.
Check the consistency; the bulgur may be chewy but
not too hard. At this point you will know if a little more
liquid is needed.

Try this marinade on soaked quinoa or cooked barley for a
lovely East meets West version of Taboulé.

OLIVE & ROSEMARY BREAD

1 kg wholemeal Spelt Flour
2 teaspoons instant Dried Yeast
4 mugs warm Water
1 mug of Green *or* Black Olives, de-pitted
5 Garlic Cloves, chopped
1 teaspoon dried Rosemary *or* 1 tablespoon fresh Rosemary
2 tablespoons Olive Oil
Pepper & Salt to taste

Mix just over half of the flour with the dried yeast, add the water and mix with a wooden spoon to make a fairly wet dough.

Set aside, covered with a damp tea towel, in the warmest spot in the kitchen *(the airing cupboard is great)*.
It will vary time wise, but allow the dough to double in size.
Knead it on a work surface with the rest of the flour until the dough becomes springy and elastic to the touch.
If the dough is still sticky it will need a little more flour.
(Good bread dough can be sliced in half and you will see small air bubbles within the dough.)

Liberally oil a large flat baking tin with olive oil, sprinkle with the olives, garlic, rosemary, salt & pepper and now press the dough firmly on top and then rub a little oil & salt into the dough. Allow it to rise again to double its size.

Bake in a pre-heated oven at 180°C for about 30 minutes, the time will depend on how thick you have made the loaf.
Remove from the oven and allow to cool before turning upside down and cutting into chunks.

It is best eaten fresh, although it keeps well, and can be popped under a hot grill to refresh that lovely garlicky aroma.

SEARED AUBERGINE, PEPPERS & COURGETTES
with fresh garlic and lemon

If you have a small Panini machine or a ridged grill pan
this is a very effective way to create mouthwatering tapas.

2 Aubergines, cut in ½ inch slices
2 Red Peppers, de-seeded, cut in quarters
2 Courgettes, spliced lengthways in ½ inch slices
Sunflower Oil

For the Dressing:
1 Lemon
1 Garlic Clove, finely chopped
½ teaspoon Salt
Lots of Black Pepper
Garden Herbs, chopped
2 tablespoons Olive Oil

Rub the vegetable slices with the sunflower oil.
Place on the hot griddle and if you are using a Panini
machine close the lid.
Allow to sear. With the griddle pan they will have to
be turned; the machine will do both sides at once.

Finish the grilling by slightly changing the position of
the slices, this will create that lovely criss cross pattern.

Lay the vegetables on a flat plate and drizzle with the
dressing. Serve chilled with a few olives and some
hummus on the side.

BEETROOT & BLACKBEAN PATE with
Seared Peppers & Chocolate Chilli Sauce

**2 mugs Black Turtle Beans, soaked in
4 mugs of Water
4 large Red Peppers, cut lengthways in sixths
4 medium cooked Beetroot, cut in small chunks
1 whole Garlic Bulb
Juice of 2 Lemons
50 grams of Dark Chocolate, melted
4 tablespoons Olive Oil**

Cook the beans in the water as in the basic method
on page 2, keeping the lovely black bean stock.

Meanwhile place peppers, beetroot and garlic on a baking
tray. Douse with the marinade and grill in a hot oven
stirring frequently. This should take around ½ an hour.
Set aside ½ the peppers for decoration.

Squeeze out the garlic flesh into a blender jug add the lemon
juice, ½ the roasted peppers, the olive oil and the cooked
marinade. Add a little bean stock, the chocolate and blend
into a creamy emulsion. Now add ¾ of the cooked beans,
the beetroot and blend well, perhaps adding a little more
bean stock. This should be very smooth. Set aside to cool.

In a saucepan, gently heat all the ingredients for the chocolate
chilli sauce, stirring continuously until the chocolate melts.

Serve the creamy pate, a few strips of seared peppers, a few
black beans and garnished with the chocolate chilli sauce.

**For the Marinade:
4 tablespoons of Sunflower Oil
4 tablespoons Balsamic Vinegar
1 teaspoon Salt
1 teaspoon Black Pepper Corns, crushed
1 teaspoon Black Mustard Seed**

**For the Sauce:
50 grams 70% Dark Chocolate
½ mug Balsamic Vinegar
½ mug Black Bean Stock
¼ teaspoon Cayenne Pepper
or ¼ teaspoon Chilli Powder
2 teaspoons Honey
2 tablespoons Olive Oil
A pinch of Salt to taste**

BORLOTTI & WILD MUSHROOM MASH

I like a more textured bean dish sometimes and it is good to know one does not always need the wiz of the power blender, just a little elbow grease and an old fashioned potato masher as long as your beans are well cooked. The latter is easy enough with Borlotti beans as they tend to be too hard, and minutes later, rather mushy.

2 mugs Borlotti Beans, soaked in
   4 mugs of Water
1 mug dried Forest Mushrooms, rinsed
2 mugs hot Water
1 Onion, chopped
Sprig of Bay
2 tablespoons Tamari
1 teaspoon Toasted Sesame Oil
100 ml Soya Cream
Pepper & Salt to taste
Olive Oil for frying

Cook the beans in the 4 mugs of water for 1 hour. Meanwhile soak the mushrooms in the hot water. Agitate a little in order to dislodge any sand, thus allowing it to sink to the base of the bowl. When cool enough to handle using your fingers, remove the mushrooms from the water, gently squeeze out the excess fluid and chop.

Fry the onion until glassy, add the mushrooms and carefully pour in the mushroom liquid, except for the last drop which will always be a little sandy. Add the bay, tamari and sesame oil and simmer to reduce the stock to the consistency of a thick soup.

Strain the beans and mash all ingredients together with the soya cream, adding a little bean stock if necessary.

Serve piping hot with lots of pepper and a drizzle of olive oil. This is surprisingly good and comforting on a wintery day with a steamed spud plonked in the centre, drizzled generously with herb oil.

For a more sophisticated and colourful dish try it contrasted with some sweet oven roast peppers, or served as a warm tapas dip with crispy chicory leaves to scoop it up.

A Simply Smashing Potato Yarn

became bitten by the travel bug in England during the early seventies and was constantly being enticed to distant shores. To finance these trips I would take on numerous occupations, in fact as many as I could fit into one day. These diverse jobs were great fun, as their existence in my life was fleeting. They were a means to an end, and the end was to be gone a.s.a.p.

I was the smiling, flirtatious bar maid, the girl who gaily dished out hospital meals from a roasting bain-marie trolley, I sold electric yo-yos in Oxford Street from an extremely dubious market stall and walked and shampooed dogs. I was the sexy voiced telephonist for a mini cab firm in Soho. I worked in a garage, filled petrol and washed windscreens; happily checking oil whilst convincing car reps, running in sparkly new vehicles, to pick me up at the end of my shift and drop me to my next port of call. I was a one woman employment agency including its entire work force, the forerunner of super woman, I was 'Super Girl'.

One of my favourite duties was cleaning for a wealthy Irish widow who lived alone in a house full of antiques and memories. After I had rattled around with the Original Hoover, waxed the furniture with a particularly soporific lavender scented polish, the lady of the house would lure me into the warmth of the kitchen. There, the Aga would be oozing with the smell of steaming potatoes and onions sizzling in butter. The room would then become alive with tales of her deceased husband, "The Physician", her beloved "Old Country"; and of her children long grown and long gone, far, far, into the West; and "The New Country" of great sky scrapers and even greater fortunes.

As the onions slowly glazed and I drifted sleepily through the lilt of her stories she would interrupt her narrative by giving cooking instructions, "use plenty of butter in order to absorb the sweet flavours" *(this was the rich golden butter from Kerry)*, "and to stop them burning... well, simply add some more". She peeled the hot potatoes miraculously without burning her hands by gently piercing them with a fork and deftly skimming off the dry papery skin, "cooking them like this keeps all the goodness within", she said, knowing this was alien to my English culinary ways. They were then mashed smooth with milk and a generous twist of salt and pepper. Finally the deliciously golden onions were added and folded in with a wooden spoon.

I may have slept and gone to heaven for there before my eyes was a mash fit for a queen. "And tomorrow I will do the same using yellow swede... and you know it's very good with turnip too... have some grated cheddar cheese with that", said she, "and will I be expecting you tomorrow then, same time!?".

The latter was more of a statement than a question and with my mouth full I could only nod blissfully.

BAKES · ROASTS · GRILLS · STIR FRYS ·

Over the years I have made simple variations with a sprinkle of nutmeg for a sophisticated flavour and aphrodisiacal properties; or a spoonful of sweet curry powder which makes the potatoes turn a sunny yellow. The latter is also great chilled and mixed through with mayonnaise, fresh chives or coriander.

Having my own agenda, one day, of course I did not return, at least never in the physical body, but if I close my eyes it is easy to feel her nearby and enjoy her presence, every time I cook Colcannon.

PUMPKINS & SQUASH

These versatile vegetables deserve pages of recipes...

- They are great in soups and stews or as a rösti and make a very delicious and comforting mash. Combined with other pureed vegetables they are a delightful and nourishing baby food.

- Try roasting in chunks or slices and tossing in a sweet spicy dressing with some fresh flat leaf parsley.

- For a simple soup, fry with an onion and a pinch of ground fenugreek. Simmer slowly in water, add seasoning, a squeeze of lemon and liquidize with some soya or dairy cream.

- For an elegant mash, steam with a few potatoes, cream together with saffron and almond milk and serve drizzled with olive oil and black pepper.

- Grate and squeeze out the excess fluid, season well and add a finely chopped onion. Fry in small rösti forms in a hot oiled pan turning over carefully in order to brown both sides, sprinkle with fresh coriander and serve with a sweet pepper salsa...

and... across the Atlantic Ocean it is served sweetened with dates and honey in a pie...
and... at The Phoenix we occasionally cook it with fresh ginger and honey to add to our fruit crumble !

BUTTERNUT SQUASH STEAKS
with Crunchy Amaranth Seed Topping

The Amaranth can be replaced with Quinoa in this recipe.

1 large Butternut Squash
Olive Oil

For the topping:
1 Onion, finely diced
1 mug of Amaranth Seed
1 mug of Water
1 mug of Sunflower Seed
Tamari, Olive Oil & black pepper

Amaranth or 'Love Lies Bleeding'

Pre heat the oven to 200°C. Slice a butternut squash into inch thick rings. Avoid the bulbous seedy end, as whole, flat surfaces are needed. Brush with oil, place on a baking tray and bake for 15 minutes.

Meanwhile, dry roast the amaranth seed in a saucepan until some start to pop. Cover in the water, a generous dash of tamari and a drizzle of oil. Continue to cook for about 5 minutes, stirring occasionally and adding more water if it becomes too dry. The seed won't really get soft but will begin to bind slightly.

Dry roast the sunflower seed, roughly grind and combine with the onion and the cooked amaranth. Remove the squash from the oven and turn over. Paste the topping generously on top, firmly pressing it down onto each ring, drizzle with olive oil & a twist of pepper.
Return to the oven for about 20 minutes to crisp up.

These steaks are delicious served on a bed of tomato sauce with a little steamed rice on the side.
They keep well semi-baked and can be reheated in a hot oven.

SWISS CHARD

I have grown Swiss Chard for as long as I can remember. For me it is a staple vegetable and I have to be careful not to use it in absolutely everything.

This can prove difficult sometimes, as we plant it in spring and it grows quickly and profusely all through the summer and autumn.

There is an abundance of varieties from dark to bright green, a rich ruby and even a pretty rainbow coloured chard. The young leaves and thinnings can be used in salad bowls while the larger stronger leaves and stems can be used in anything from lovely dark green soups and stews and as an added flavour to bakes, patties and pancakes.

The stems can be separated and are delicious sprinkled with olive oil and baked. Our Basque friend and chef, Inaki, dips the stems in a tempura batter, fries them and serves them with a dipping sauce.

Chard grows rather like a bi-annual and will have a new spurt of life in late winter before bolting in April. They can be planted as early as February and as late as September. It is therefore, the one thing I literally, have growing all year round, and what could be better for our bodies than a garden fresh vegetable that is so readily available.

STUFFED RED PEPPERS
with Parsnips & Walnuts

5-6 Red Peppers
1 mug Parsnip, grated
½ mug of cooked, mashed Potato
1 mug Walnuts
½ mug Sunflower Seed
¼ mug Polenta Meal
2 mugs Water
100 grams Silken Tofu
2 Onions, diced
2 tablespoons Tamari
½ teaspoon Salt
Black Pepper
2 tablespoons Olive Oil

For the Dressing:
A generous dash of Olive Oil
Balsamic Vinegar
Salt & Pepper

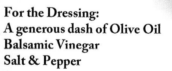

In a frying pan, lightly dry roast the walnuts and sunflower seed, stir in the tamari and remove from the heat.
Mix the onion and parsnip together with the polenta meal, the potatoes and mashed tofu.
Season and add 1 tablespoon of olive oil; it will be slightly sloppy, bear in mind that the polenta is not yet cooked.

Cut the tops off the red peppers, de-seed them and fill with the mixture. Sprinkle generously with the dressing, cover with foil and bake at 150°C, gas mark 5, for at least 1 hour.

The peppers will keep for 2-4 days
in the fridge. They can be served hot
or cold, and when reheating, remove the
tops of the peppers to prevent burning.

Serve:
Hot - with tangy chutney and steamed vegetables
Warm - with spicy grilled apples
Cold - with balsamic dipping sauce and lamb's tongue lettuce

Winter 2009

SAVOURY WALNUT ROAST

This roast is ideal for freezing, so it is worth making the full amount and popping half in the freezer for that special occasion.

I am often asked to supply foods for students to take back to college, this is a fantastic protein packed "meal in a slice".

For the Lentil Mixture:

1 mug Mung Beans, sprouted in 2 mugs of water for 12 hours

1 mug Brown Lentils, pre-soaked in 2 mugs of water for a minimum of 1 hour

6 Cloves of Garlic, chopped

4 large Onions, diced

3 Red Peppers, diced

4 Sticks Celery, diced

2 medium Carrots, diced

2 tins Organic Chopped Tomatoes

100 ml Water

100 ml White Wine

2 teaspoons Piri-Piri

2 teaspoons Mixed Herbs

3 teaspoons Salt

A good twist of Black Pepper

1 teaspoon Tumeric

1 mug Polenta Flour

1 mug Quinoa Flakes

4 tablespoons of Sunflower Oil for frying

For the Nutty Mixture:

2 teaspoons Coriander Seeds, crushed

4 mugs Walnuts, chopped

1 mug Green Pumpkin Seeds, lightly chopped

1 mug Dried Apricots, chopped, medium fine

3 tablespoons Agave Syrup *(or any sweet syrup)*

4 tablespoons Tamari

1 tablespoon Olive Oil

1-2 Sweet Potatoes, finely sliced into strips
   with a peeler for lining the dish

Lentil Mixture

In a large saucepan, fry the garlic and onions
until golden. Add the rest of the vegetables
and continue to sauté for 5 minutes.
Combine the tomatoes, seasoning, water, wine,
the sprouted mung beans and the lentils
including the liquid they have been soaked in.
Cook on a low heat, stirring occasionally until
the pulses have just softened.
This will take about 20 minutes.
Remove from the heat and rest for 5 minutes.
Stir in the Polenta and the Quinoa Flakes and
stir vigorously.

Nutty Mixture

In a little oil, lightly fry the walnuts, pumpkin
seeds, apricots and coriander, then add the
Agave syrup and Tamari.
Stir well and then remove instantly from the
heat to prevent burning.

BAKING METHOD:

Line 2 x 4lb loaf tins with greaseproof paper. Layer each tin with
the sweet potato strips letting them overlap the sides.
Fill just under ½ the tins with the lentil mixture, add the nutty
mixture per tin and then cover with the lentil mixture.
Firmly press everything down with the palm of the hand and fold
the overlapped sweet potato strips over the top.

If you are using a ceramic dish omit the greaseproof paper.
This roast may also be made in single portion ramekins.

Bake at 180°C for 1 hour or until firm to the touch. If you are
making it in advance in order to reheat then slightly
under-cook the roast.

Carefully up turn the roast onto a dish and serve like a traditional
roast dinner resplendent with crispy vegetables and gravy.
It keeps very well in a fridge for at least 5 days.

SPLIT GREEN PEA, SWISS CHARD & PUMPKIN BAKE

**2 mugs of dried Split Green Peas, soaked in
  4 mugs of Water**
2 large Onions, chopped
2 Potatoes, diced
1 small Red Pumpkin, cut into small cubes
1 large colander of Swiss Chard, chopped
1 mug Sunflower Seed
1 mug Sesame Seed
½ mug of Linseed
Tamari
Sunflower Oil for frying & roasting
Salt & Pepper

This dish has a lovely textured top with the orange pumpkin and the toasted seeds. The combination of split green peas and potato are sticky enough to hold this light and very tasty bake together.

Cook the split peas slowly in the soaking water for about 50 minutes, until soft. Stir occasionally as these tend to stick more than other pulses.

Lightly oven roast the red pumpkin in a little oil.

Meanwhile fry the onion with the potatoes and when almost cooked add the chard and continue to cook for about 5 minutes. Season well.

Dry roast the sunflower seed in a frying pan and when hot add the sesame and linseed, continue to heat until the sesame seeds start to crackle. Stirring briskly, douse in tamari and remove from the heat.

When cool, coarsely grind the seeds in a food processor and then mix together with the pumpkin cubes.
Place the green pea and spinach mix into an oiled baking dish and top with the seed and pumpkin mix.
Bake at 200°C. for 30 minutes.

Serve as a light lunch with a vegetable salad and a salsa, or as a dinner with some steamed rice and a rich tomato sauce.

SHEPHERDS PIE
with Green Pea Mash

When using pulses in a recipe it can be convenient and economical to prepare more than you need. Cooked, or even simply soaked, they can then be refrigerated or frozen and used in a variety of dishes such as soups, dips, bakes and stews.

2 medium Leeks, chopped
1 colander of Spinach or Chard, lightly chopped
2 tablespoons Potato Flour
1 mug of non-dairy Milk
Salt & Pepper
Sunflower Oil for frying

For the Topping:
4 mugs of cooked Split Peas
½ mug non-dairy Milk
4 Potatoes, steamed
The juice & zest of 1 Lemon
A little grated Nutmeg
Salt & Pepper
3 tablespoons of Olive Oil

Lightly fry the leeks in sunflower oil, add the spinach and allow to wilt and then season. Whisk the potato flour into 1 mug of milk until lump free and then stir into the leek mixture and simmer until the sauce thickens.

Using a blender, liquidize the split peas. Mash the potatoes with ½ a mug of milk, olive oil, the lemon juice and zest, salt, black pepper, nutmeg and then combine with the pureed peas.

Place the creamed vegetable mixture in a baking dish. Spread the pea & mash mixture on top. Bake in a hot oven until the topping is slightly crispy.

This comforting bake resembles a creamy green shepherd's pie.

Non vegetarians really love it, and it looks stunning with a bright red beetroot salad and sweet, spicy chutney on the side.

85

GRILLED AUBERGINE STEAKS with a Puy Lentil Topping

2 Aubergines
2 Tomatoes, sliced
2 mugs Puy Lentils, soaked in 4 mugs of Water
2 Onions, finely diced
Bunch of fresh Dill Herb, finely chopped
2 teaspoons Yellow Mustard Seed
Juice of 1 Lemon
2 tablespoons Balsamic Vinegar
2 tablespoons Pumpkin Seed Oil
1 teaspoon Salt
A generous twist of Black Pepper
Sunflower Oil, for grilling and for baking tray

Cook the lentils in the water with the yellow mustard seed. They should be soft and sticky enough so that they hold together. Allow to cool slightly.

Place the finely diced onions on a large board, sprinkle with the salt and the lemon juice and re-chop in order to make a paste. Add the onion mix, pumpkin seed oil, dill and pepper to the lentils.

Meanwhile cut the aubergines into ½ inch diagonals and place on an oiled baking tray. Sprinkle with salt, a drizzle of oil and the balsamic vinegar, then grill for roughly 5 minutes per side on a high heat.

Place the warm lentil mixture on top of each ring in a firm heap, top with a slice of tomato and re-grill on a slightly lower heat. When the tomato is cooked so are the steaks. Remove carefully with a large spatula.

Serve piping hot, or warm, as a main course with some grilled fennel. It could also be served chilled as a starter course, with a sweet balsamic dressing and garnished with fresh fennel.

Fennel herb, which tends to be available most times of the year in the garden, can replace the fresh dill.

POLENTA SLICE with Pan Fried Leek

1 mug Medium Ground Polenta
4 mugs of boiling Water
1 teaspoon Salt
2 large Leeks, coarsely sliced
2 firm Pears or Apples, cut into chunks
Sunflower Seeds
Tamari
Fresh Chives, chopped
Nutmeg
Generous twist of Pepper
Sunflower Oil for frying
Olive Oil for the flan dish

Cook the polenta by simmering the salted water and slowly pouring in the polenta whilst vigorously beating with a strong balloon whisk.
Cover and simmer on a low heat for about 5 minutes.

Meanwhile fry the leeks in oil at a high temperature. They should turn slightly golden yet retain some bite. Add the fruit, fry for a minute longer and combine with the polenta, check the seasoning and simmer together for a further couple of minutes.

Lightly oil a round flan dish and sprinkle with sunflower seeds, chives, pepper, a swirl of tamari and a generous grating of nutmeg. Using a large soup ladle, spoon the mixture into the flan dish, allow to cool and set.

Serving suggestion:

When cool cut into sections. Splice and butterfly each section and pop under a very hot grill. Serve sizzling with grilled tofu or goat's cheese wedged between the slices.

This polenta can also be served straight from the pan with a rich tomato sauce, monika beans *(see page 102)* or any chilli.

If served this way the consistency is that of a soft mash.

Cooked polenta keeps well for several days in the fridge and can be grilled, baked or fried when re-heating.

Alternatives:

Instead of the leek, fry an onion and add spinach or chard, or in Autumn it is lovely to use pumpkin, butternut squash and green baby tomatoes which are a very juicy and unusual addition to the polenta.

MILLET HERB BAKE
with Swiss Chard & Creamy Tofu Topping

1 mug Millet
1 mug Mung Beans, soaked in 4 mugs of Water
2 large Onions, finely sliced
2 medium Carrots, chopped
1 medium Sweet Potato, chopped
A colander of Chard or Spinach, chopped
½ teaspoon Salt
A good twist of Pepper
2 tablespoons of Sunflower Oil for frying

For the Topping:
300 grams Silken Tofu
A good handful of Seasonal Fresh Herbs
1 mug of non-dairy Milk
1 tablespoon Corn Flour or Potato Flour
1 tablespoon Olive Oil
Salt & Pepper

In a saucepan dry roast the millet with the salt until hot to
the touch. Add the mung beans, water and once boiling,
reduce the heat, cover and simmer for 20 minutes.

In a large wok lightly fry the onion, carrot and sweet potato,
adding the spinach at very the end. Combine with the
cooked millet and mung bean mix, add the pepper, check
the seasoning and spread the mixture into a well oiled
ceramic baking dish.

Liquidize all the topping ingredients
together. It should have a thick, pourable
consistency. Spread over the bake.

Bake in a pre-heated oven at 200°C for
20-30 minutes, until the topping is
slightly golden.

Serve with a tomato sauce and a cooked
beetroot and chicory winter salsa.

Note: This bake will keep several days in
the fridge and may be frozen in pieces.
Alternatively the bake can be prepped
and assembled a day in advance.

The baking time will be doubled
if the bake is cooked from cold.

If there is any tomato hummus left over
in the fridge I will often use this to replace
some of the tofu in the topping.
This gives a warm pink glow to the bake.

For added protein and a lighter texture
replace ½ the millet with quinoa.
The mung beans can be substituted with
green or brown puy lentils.

MILLET CAKES with Swiss Chard & Walnuts

Large bunch of Chard
1 mug Millet
½ mug Quinoa
3 mugs Water
2 medium Onions
1 mug Walnuts, chopped
½ teaspoon Dried Rosemary
A good twist of Ground Pepper
½ teaspoon Salt
A generous dollop of Olive Oil

Remove the green chard leaves from the stems. Finely chop the onions and the chard stems, and using a large saucepan lightly fry in olive oil.

Add the millet & quinoa and stir to coat the grain, then add the water and salt. Cook for 15 minutes. Chop the greens, and gently stir into the grain, cover and rest the mixture.

Mix the rosemary and walnuts together and season with salt and pepper. Brush a bun tray with sunflower oil and sprinkle the sections with ½ the nutty mixture. Fill with the cooked grain mixture and top with the remaining nuts, gently pressing them down.

Bake the cakes in a medium oven for as long as it takes to brown the nuts; 15-20 minutes. Remove from the heat and allow to cool a little before gently prizing them from the baking cups.

Serve warm, popped on top of a salad sprinkled with coconut chutney as a light lunch *or* on top of a vegetable stew for a winter warmer.

As an alternative to the chard, walnut and rosemary, try grated carrots, cashew nuts and fresh coriander.

OVEN ROAST PUMPKIN
with Honey & Garlic Dressing

This recipe couldn't be simpler, and the white wine vinegar enhances the pumpkin's fiery colour.

1 medium Red Kuri Pumpkin
2 tablespoons White Wine Vinegar
Salt & Black Pepper
2 tablespoons Olive oil

For the Dressing:
Juice of 1 Lemon
2 Garlic Cloves, crushed
2 teaspoons Honey
¼ teaspoon Salt
A pinch of Cayenne Pepper

Cut 6 half inch slices of the pumpkin lengthways following its natural moon like shape.

Brush generously with olive oil and white wine vinegar, sprinkle with salt and pepper, place on a baking tray and pop into a hot oven at 200°C.
Turn the slices after 15 minutes and return to the oven for a further 10 minutes or until the colour changes and they form a slightly crispy surface.

Remove from the oven. place in a serving dish and drizzle with the dressing.

For a real Mexican theme, the slices are lovely served with a dark red spicy bean stew with some lightly steamed quinoa on the side.

OVEN ROAST VEGETABLES
with Chickpeas

Artichoke hearts can be bought fresh and then steamed and peeled down to the heart. Conveniently they are easily sourced tinned or jarred in brine.

1 mug cooked Chickpeas
1 Sweet Potato, cut in chunks
1 Onion, large slices
1 Celeriac, cut in chunks
1 Red Pepper, large slices
5 Artichoke Hearts, drained and halved
1 whole Garlic Bulb

For the Marinade:
2 tablespoons Balsamic Vinegar
2 tablespoons Red Wine Vinegar
A small bunch of Rosemary & Seasonal Herbs
1 teaspoon Cumin Seed
½ teaspoon Salt
A generous twist of Black Pepper
¼ mug Olive Oil

Place the vegetables and the garlic bulb into a large baking dish and douse with the marinade.
Bake in a hot oven at 200°C, stirring occasionally, for about 30 minutes until the vegetables soften and then add the chickpeas.

Squeeze out the softened garlic cloves into a little oil, mash and stir into the vegetables. Serve with a robust pasta such as large tri-coloured shells. There are many new varieties of rice pasta available which lend themselves well to this kind of chunky vegetable dish. This also works well cold as a nourishing pasta salad for a picnic on a hot summer's day.

RED CABBAGE cooked in Wine with Prunes

This is a winter classic; crimson, tart, and warming.
Lovely with colcannon mash and baby falafels.

1 medium Red Cabbage, shredded
1 Onion, diced
2 Apples, chopped
100 grams Stoned Prunes, chopped
1 mug Red Wine
2 mugs Water
1 teaspoon Fenugreek Powder
1 teaspoon Salt
A generous twist of Pepper
Sunflower Oil for frying

In a large pan, fry the onion then add the fenugreek powder.

Add the cabbage, wine, apples, prunes and water.
Season well and allow to simmer for at least 1 hour, first
with the lid on, then with the lid off - to thoroughly reduce.
The cabbage should be soft and juicy; swimming in a sweet,
thick liquid.

A great addition, or alternative, to the prunes, are cooked
chestnuts. Add them when you would normally add the
prunes. Vacuum packed chestnuts are succulent and usually
of good quality.
Sweet curry powder can replace the fenugreek.

POK CHOI STIR FRY
with Mushrooms

Success with a vegetable stir fry depends on knowing the length of time it takes to cook each type of vegetable. Ideally the vegetables are piping hot, cooked and sealed on the outside and crunchy on the inside.
Pok choi is a lesser used vegetable which also works well in a strong salad.
In this case it only needs a fleeting visit to the hot wok.

1 Pok Choi, cut in ½ inch slices
1 large Carrot, sliced in diagonal slithers, ¼ inch thick
1 Onion, chopped into ¼ inch slices
3 large Field Mushrooms, cut into chunky strips
4 Garlic Cloves, diced
2-3 tablespoons Sunflower Oil for frying

For the Marinade:
A knob of Fresh Ginger, diced
Squeeze of Lemon
2-3 tablespoons Tamari
1 teaspoon Toasted Sesame Oil
Dash of Soya Cream
Salt & Pepper to taste

Combine the ingredients for the marinade. Heat a large wok. When good and hot add the sunflower oil, swirl it around and quickly toss in all the vegetables apart from the Pok Choi.
Keeping the heat full on, stir stir stir !

When everything is sizzling, stir in the Pok Choi and then toss in the marinade and cook for barely a minute.

Serve to your waiting family or guests with steamed rice or noodles. This dish is *all* in the preparation, which can be done well in advance. The actual cooking time is only around 5 minutes.

Alternative vegetables, pre-cooked pulses, seeds and fruits may be used.

PAN FRIED SMOKED TOFU with Garden Fresh Spinach

We plant an abundance of spinach in early spring as ground cover in our tunnels. It provides us with tasty, nutritious early greens and acts as a green fertilizer by replenishing the soil with nitrogen. Then, as the weather heats up it starts to bolt and there is a race to use it all up.

200 grams Smoked Tofu
A colander of Spinach, washed, *tough stems removed*
2 tablespoons Sunflower Oil for frying

For the Marinade:
1 thumb sized knob of fresh Ginger, coarsely grated
2 Garlic Cloves, pressed
Juice of 1 Lemon
2 tablespoons Tamari
Salt & Black Pepper

For the Garnish:
½ mug Sesame Seed
Fresh Coriander Leaves
A wedge of Lemon

Cut the tofu into sturdy strips, soak in the marinade and set aside for a minimum of 30 minutes. In a wok, heat the sunflower oil, drain off excess marinade from the tofu and fry, allowing it to seal before gently turning; this should take a few minutes on each side. Add the spinach to the wok and fry until it is just wilted yet still retains its bright green colour.

Meanwhile, dry roast the sesame seeds until they start to crackle. Sprinkle them on top of the greens along with the coriander and lemon. This dish is perfect served with steamed wholemeal rice and spicy grilled apples. It also works well as a warm salad, in which case add a squeeze of lime and toss it together with a handful of succulent baby tomatoes.

CARROT & COURGETTE SLITHERS
with Spinach

2 long Carrots
1-2 small Courgettes
1 colander of tender young Chard Leaves *or* **Spinach**
1 Garlic Clove, chopped
1 tablespoon Sesame Seed
1 small Chillie Pepper, finely diced
Sunflower Oil for frying

For the Marinade:
2 tablespoons of Olive Oil
Juice of 1 Lemon
1 teaspoon of Toasted Sesame Oil
Pepper & Salt

Using a Swiss potato peeler slither the carrots and courgette into long strips.

Drizzle on the marinade, stir and set aside to soften. Lightly fry the garlic, chillie and sesame seeds until golden. Steam the spinach or chard until wilted.

Toss all ingredients together and serve slightly warm. The carrots and courgettes will remain a little perky as they are uncooked.

To give this a more Asian feel add some finely chopped ginger, a dash of tamari and a little zest of lime.

This dish can be used as a structural garnish on top of a bake or a pasta dish.

SPICY GRILLED APPLES

6 medium Apples
2 mugs of Baby Tomatoes, ripe & green
2 tablespoons of warmed Honey

For the Dressing:
½ mug Balsamic Vinegar
¼ mug Olive Oil
¼ teaspoon Salt
A pinch of Cayenne Pepper

From August on we have an abundance of apples
and baby tomatoes, both red and yellow.
This is a lovely and a very easy way to use them up.

Core and chunk the apples and place them in a
baking tray with the tomatoes.
Add the dressing and stir to coat.

Pop under a pre-heated grill until golden and
sizzling. This will take 5-10 minutes.

Place the mixture in a large bowl and pour the
warmed honey over the apples.

Serve warm with a celeriac frittata or use cold
as a mouth watering condiment.

As an alternative to the tomatoes use red or
yellow peppers cut into chunky strips

This dish keeps very well in an airtight container
in the fridge for at least 5 days.

A *Little Bit of* Monica Beans

hilst in Switzerland we lived in an archaic and ramshackle farmhouse surrounded by grazing sheep, abundant fruit trees and fields of hay or maize.

In winter, the adjacent hills were white with snow, haw frosts bejewelled the trees and the childrens' red cheeks matched their snow suits as they learnt to ski and sledge at breakneck speed.

The Benedictine nuns at the impeccable fourteenth century convent baked the Communion Host for the surrounding churches. Compassionately we were given great bags of left over cuttings from their baking "for our rabbits" and once discreetly, a recipe for what was effectively 'Body of Christ' soup.

Even though I had far too many children for the native Swiss population and a bizarre habit of belly dancing at local events, we existed very happily on the razor's edge of village society.

For a while we had a beautiful Brazilian au pair called Monica. On sultry afternoons, dressed in tiny florescent triangles which she generously called a bikini, Monica would sunbathe in our garden. On those days the fields next to us became a hive of activity, teeming with local farmers, who were hardly optimizing their work force, with as many as three or more men per tractor.

Monica could cook two things; one was white rice, the other red beans. The rice was fairly straight forward but the beans were rather special:

Soak red kidney beans for a several hours, change the water and cook until almost soft. Meanwhile, take lots of onions and some dried or fresh chillies; finely chop and fry in plenty of olive oil, pepper, rosemary and thyme. The onions must become slightly crispy. Add to the beans with a generous pinch of salt and reduce for about another 30 minutes, until the beans are completely cooked and have absorbed most of the liquid. Stir, but don't mash; these are not refried beans.

Serve with white rice, some grated cheese, finely chopped tomatoes and a little bit of...

Hermetschwil 1988

102

MONICA BEANS
in Tomato Sauce

4 mugs cooked Red Kidney Beans
1 jar Passata
  or 2 tins Chopped Tomatoes
2 large Red Onions, diced
2 dried Chillies, diced
Sprig each of Rosemary and Thyme
2 Bay Leaves
4 squares Dark Chocolate
Salt & Pepper
Olive Oil for the garnish
Sunflower Oil for frying

In a large pan fry the onions and chillies in the sunflower oil until they almost start to crisp. Add the thyme, rosemary, bay, the tomatoes, cooked beans with plenty of the thick bean stock. Season well and reduce for a further 30 minutes, stirring frequently.
When almost finished add the chocolate, olive oil and adjust the seasoning.

Serve with rice, a creamy dip and warm tortillas or as a small side dish to a rösti. The beans keep surprisingly well for about 5 days in the fridge.

THREE BEAN CHILLI

Comforting, nourishing food, with strong flavours and textures. The quantities below are enough for a large party, especially when you don't know how many people will show up, or when. Great for around a bonfire.

1 mug Cannelloni Beans, soaked
1 mug Kidney Beans, soaked
1 mug Aduki Beans, soaked
A sprig of Bay
2 Onions, chopped
1 whole Garlic Bulb, peeled and chopped
2 Red Chillies
1 teaspoon Cumin Seed
4 Red Peppers, chopped
4 Carrots, chopped
2 Sweet Potatoes, chopped
1 Celeriac, chopped
2 tins Chopped Tomatoes *or*
  8 fresh Tomatoes, chopped
200ml Soya Cream
Fresh Sage, Thyme & Rosemary
Salt & Black Pepper to taste
¼ mug Sunflower Oil for frying

Change the bean water after soaking. Boil all the beans in a large pan with plenty of water and some dried or fresh bay.

The beans will take 1 hour to cook until completely soft.

Meanwhile, fry the garlic, chillies and cumin until the garlic begins to turn golden. Add the onion and continue to fry until they soften.

Add all the other vegetables, herbs and seasoning and gently cook with a lid on. Combine the cooked vegetables and cooked beans and reduce together for about 5 minutes. Adjust seasoning and just before serving add the cream.

This dish is a meal in its own right, served with bread to mop up the lovely sauce or some crispy corn tortillas to dip and scoop up the hearty stew.

Aduki Beans

Black Turtle Beans

Red Kidney Beans

Canelloni Beans

TURTLE BEAN, TOMATO & BROCCOLI STEW

There is a fine line between a soup and a stew. The difference for me is that a soup is an appetizer and a stew serves as a meal - perhaps accompanied by some grain or potato.

**2 mugs Black Turtle Beans, soaked in
  4 mugs of Water**
2 large Onions, diced
2 Garlic Cloves, diced
2 Chillies, diced
1 Celery Stick, chopped
2 Carrots, chopped
3 Broccoli Heads, in florets
6 fresh Tomatoes, skinned & chopped
Dash of Red Wine
A handful of fresh Garden Herbs
Salt & Pepper
¼ mug of Olive & Sunflower Oil, mixed

In a large pan, fry the onion, garlic and chilli in the oil. Add the tomato, celery, carrot and the wine and cook for 10 minutes. Add the beans and the water and cook for 30 minutes, or until soft.

Season with garden herbs such as oregano, rosemary, thyme and bay, and if you have it, fresh lovage. Add salt and pepper to taste.

Add the broccoli florets and simmer without agitating too much, as the broccoli should stay whole.

Serve alone, or for a complete Mexican feel, with cheeky yellow gnocchi as dumplings.

Most bean dishes go well with tomatoes. For both their taste and colour, it is so hard to omit them. However many people do have a tomato allergy and if you are a sufferer of joint problems it is best to avoid them.

This dish works well by replacing the tomatoes with some chopped beetroot, which gives sweetness and colour.

The Definitive Dhal

Although I had been regularly utilizing pulses to thicken a vegetable stew for years, I did not appreciate the full value of the humble lentil, until my first visit to India.

I was at a friend's house in the heart of Old Delhi. We had just completed a dance class with a group of teenage girls, who had been learning the routine of the latest Bollywood blockbuster.

That same evening there was a dinner party planned; consequently the cook was knee-deep in exotic vegetables with rakes of little woks, all simmering away on any available work and floor space, in the miniscule kitchen.

"Dhal far simpler than one imagines", my Brahmin hostess assured me; shooing the children away and wading into the cooking area, her beautiful sari flowing dangerously over the naked flames. There were a few commands in Hindi and suddenly we were both squatting next to an empty burner, with a heavy bottomed pan and a bowl of washed, red lentils.

"First dry roast the spices - cumin, mustard seed, cardamon, fenugreek, and perhaps a little cinnamon for sweetness." While they were still roasting she pounded them with a wooden pestle, "do not over-roast, or they will become bitter, just enough to release the flavours". She then added Ghee *(traditionally clarified butter which may be replaced with oil)* and a handful of chopped onions.

"Fry these until the onions are golden. If you like it spicy fry in some chopped chillies now". She then added the lentils, extra water, a teaspoon of Haldi *(Turmeric)* and simmered it for about ten minutes, stirring and chatting away, in two languages.

"Sometimes we add some finely chopped carrot, potato or tomato, depending on what else we are serving with the meal... and of course, there are many different pulses - one can use Aduki beans, Mung beans, Urid dhal and *Chana* or Chickpea dhal; the dark brown lentils are especially good for you British as they create a meaty flavour", she said, forgetting, I was a vegetarian by choice.

Another Hindi command and the cook handed her small stainless steel bowls, bearing chopped coriander, grated coconut and ginger. "Only add salt when the lentils are cooked", she said, as she threw in the fresh herbs, "and always save a sprig of coriander for the pungent aroma when serving the dhal". She gave a final stir.

"If you are having dry curries, then make it more like a gravy." She snapped her fingers and the cook produced, as if from nowhere, a perfect Chapatti *(a flat, Indian, yeast free bread)*. We tore it into pieces, carefully only using our right hand and scooped up the deliciously creamy and slightly runny dhal, gorgeous! Simple food at its best, my hostess glanced at the cook, as if to say, now **this** is The Definitive Dhal. Oblivious of the peelings and the simmering pans, she stood, adjusted her still pristine sari, and sailed out of the kitchen. 'Ready Steady Cook' - get a life!

INDIAN CURRIES & DHALS

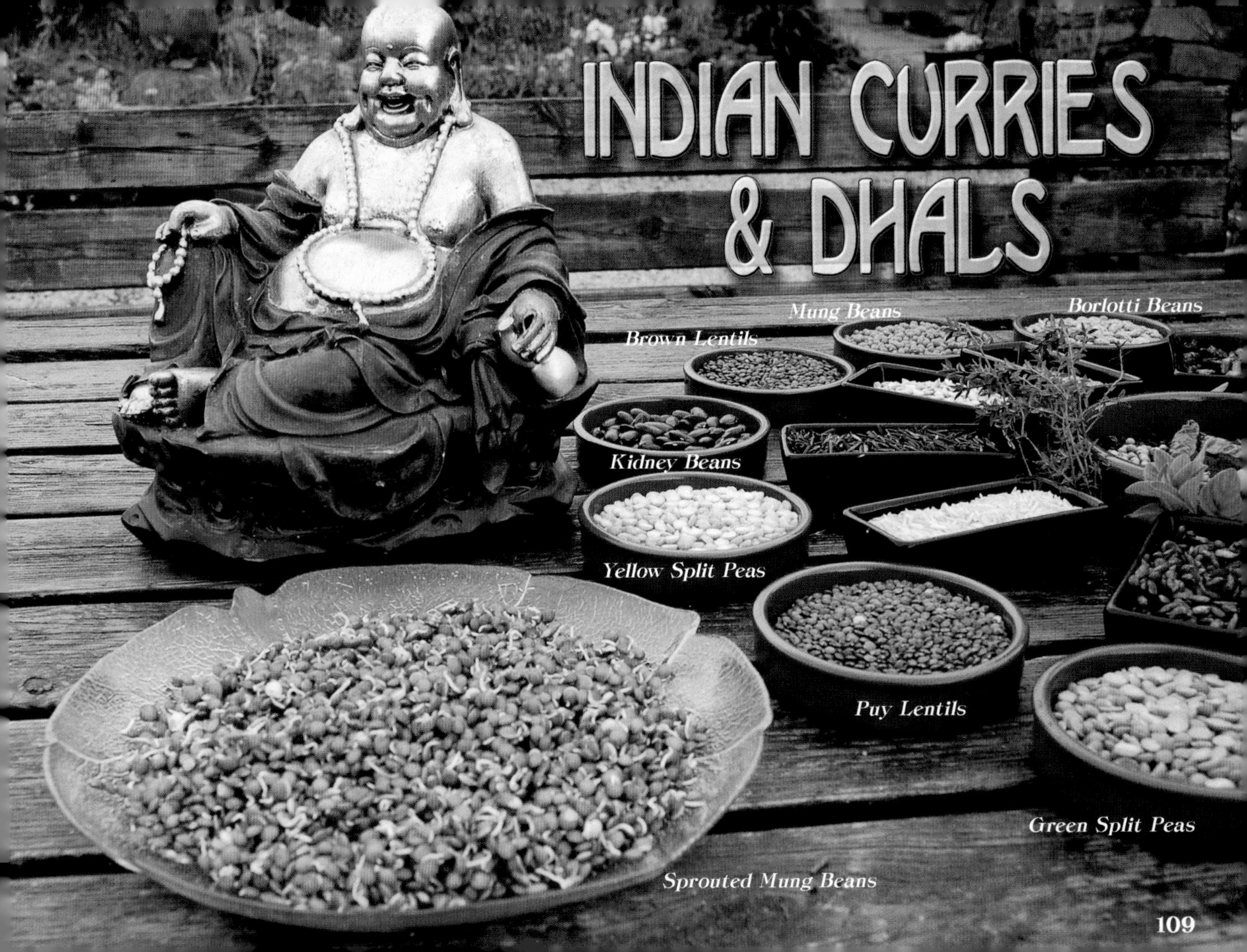

Brown Lentils

Mung Beans

Borlotti Beans

Kidney Beans

Yellow Split Peas

Puy Lentils

Green Split Peas

Sprouted Mung Beans

AUBERGINE & TOFU CURRY

In India, buffalo cheese is used in certain curries. It gives a lovely chewy texture to, for example, a creamy spinach curry or *Sag Paneer*. Tofu can replicate buffalo cheese and when lightly sautéed it becomes similar in consistency.
The Indian word for aubergine is *Brinjal*, and the buffalo cheese is called *Paneer*.

2 Aubergines
2 teaspoons Salt
1 mug Green Lentils, soaked in 2 mugs of Water
250 grams Tofu
2 Onions, finely diced
1 Carrot, finely diced
1 Apple, de-cored and chopped
Tin of Creamed Coconut
1 teaspoon whole Cumin
1 teaspoon whole Coriander
1 teaspoon whole Yellow Mustard
1 teaspoon whole Nigella
4 Cardamon Pods, husks removed
2 whole dried Chillies
Thumb sized knob of fresh Ginger, finely diced
1 teaspoon Sweet Curry Powder
4 tablespoons Coconut *or* Sunflower Oil for frying

Chop the aubergines into chunky pieces, place in a colander and sprinkle with the salt. This will help remove bitter juices and keeps the aubergines more intact when cooking.

Dry roast the whole spices until they feel hot to the touch and they begin to exude an aroma. Take care not to over roast as the spices can become bitter when over-heated.

Add the sunflower oil, the onion and carrot and fry at a low temperature.

Slice the tofu into ½ inch chunks, add to the pan and fry until the tofu swells slightly and seals.

Add the lentils and their water, the coconut, the sweet curry powder, the apples and chillies *(the chillies may be removed later and presented to someone who likes it hot)*.
Allow the lentils to cook for 5 minutes.

Shake the excess salty moisture off the aubergines and add to the pan. The curry should simmer happily for about 30 minutes. Occasionally stir and check the liquid - top up if necessary. At the very end of the cooking time stir in the fresh ginger.

This curry keeps well, even improving after a day.
When reheating always add a little water to the pan to prevent burning.

Serve with whole grain basmati rice, a sweet spicy chutney and cooling creamy cucumber raita.

SWEET POTATO & CHICK PEA CURRY with Smoked Tofu

Not every curry has to be served in a thick creamy sauce. This curry has a lovely deep sweetness, enhanced by the smokey tofu. The chickpeas and the sunny orange of the sweet potato create added texture and colour. We use several tofu recipes in the restaurant; tofu is fun to use and it is really a very easy product to source and keep in readiness in your fridge.

200 grams Smoked Tofu, cubed
(save the smokey liquid it comes in)

2 large Sweet Potatoes, cubed

2 mugs cooked Chickpeas

2 Onions, finely diced

1 Carrot, finely diced

1 Red Pepper, cut into large slices

2 tablespoons dried Apricots, chopped

½ teaspoon Turmeric

2-4 dried *or* fresh Chillies

½ teaspoon Cumin Seed

½ teaspoon Coriander Seed

½ teaspoon Yellow Mustard Seed

1-2 Cinnamon Sticks *or* 1 teaspoon of powder

1-2 whole Star Anise, *(may be removed after cooking)*

2-4 dried, frozen *or* fresh Lime Leaves

Juice of ½ Lime

A good dash of Tamari

½ mug Desiccated Coconut

1 teaspoon Salt

4 tablespoons Coconut *or* Sunflower Oil for frying

Lightly dry roast all the whole spices in a wok. Add the oil, chillies, onion and turmeric. Sauté slowly, add the tofu and allow it to cook and absorb the flavours. Tofu swells when cooked and if sautéed it will form a skin, this is what you want in order for it to keep its shape and texture.

Add the vegetables, fruit and chickpeas. Once all the vegetables are roasting hot, dash them with tamari and up to ½ a mug of water add the lime juice and lime leaves, as well as the smokey flavoured liquid from the tofu.

Add the coconut and salt then cook until tender for roughly 30 minutes. Add a little water if the mixture starts to become too dry. Remove from the heat and cover until you are ready to serve.

Serve with a runny dhal and a crispy fresh vegetable chutney. This curry keeps well in the fridge for 3-4 days.

Green Split Pea Dhal
with Seeds

Ten A Day Salad
with Tomato Pesto

Red Lentil Dahl
with Green Pesto

Rich Tomato
Sauce with Pesto

STUFFED FIELD MUSHROOMS

I travelled to Istanbul to dance with Neserin Topkapi. The elegant minarets, the mosques and the palatial harems shone majestically before my eyes. The people were warm and friendly and the food was delicious - including appetizing stuffed tomatoes, aubergines and peppers of all shapes, cabbage, spinach and vine leaves wrapped around rice; so exciting for a dancing vegetarian on the go.

Of all the ingredients for stuffing vegetables, the pulses seem to do the trick fantastically. So if you ever have dahls or beans left over it is so easy to create a colourful dish of scrumptious delights. Here the mushrooms give a succulent yet solid base.

6 large Field Mushrooms, washed, stalks removed
3 mugs of Dahl or Chilli, mashed with a fork
2 Spring Onions, chopped
A few Cherry Tomatoes
A drizzle of Tamari
A sprinkle of Balsamic Vinegar
Black Pepper & Salt
Olive oil

Oil a baking tray, place the mushrooms on top, upside down; sprinkle with salt and pepper. Combine the onion and mashed pulse, firmly pressing the mixture onto the mushrooms; decorate with the tomatoes, drizzle in oil, tamari and balsamic vinegar, and bake in a hot oven.

Serve on toast for breakfast, or at midnight... after a night of dancing.

DHAL

Dhal is an Indian word meaning a sauce or gravy made with a pulse. A very basic and speedy one is a red lentil dhal. It can be as simple as dry roasting a few spices, adding washed lentils and water and cooking until soft and mushy, then seasoning well. Most other pulses must be soaked, as in the Basic Pulse Method on page 2, before using in a Dhal.

In pure Brahmin cookery, onions and garlic are not used as they are said to raise the blood heat and allow emotional passions to rise… "bring on the onions"!
A replacement spice which is extremely pungent and must be used sparingly, is Asafoetida and the fairly bitter Fenugreek. Both these spices feature in Indian natural medicine.

Indian cookery can be rich with clarified butter or ghee. This is used in the Northen Provinces and the more arable areas where there is plenty of grazing. In the Southern or drier regions, coconut oil tends to replace ghee.
The advantage of both these fats is the high temperature they can reach without burning. A sunflower frying oil may easily replace both these fats. Oils and fats work as flavour enhancers by absorbing the natural essential essences through heat, improving the flavours in order to really excite the taste buds.

Kids tend to love a basic non-spicy dhal, simply served with a dash of tamari, a knob of butter or a drizzle of olive oil.

Dhal keeps well in the fridge. It will set when cold and can then be used as a spread and it is the easiest thing in the world to turn it into a nutritious soup.

Pulses are all complex carbohydrates and release energy into the blood stream over a sustained period. When they are eaten together with nuts, seeds, whole grains or dairy products they become a richer source of protein.

In some countries, such as India and Sri Lanka, dhal is a staple food and is served with rice and curry or just chapattis to scoop it up.
A traditional mixed tali plate always contains more than one dhal.

114

MUNG BEAN & LEEK DHAL

Mung beans are best soaked, even if only for half an hour in warm water. They begin the sprouting process really quickly and I love to set some aside to sprinkle on a salad or a stir fry. They keep well in a container in the fridge for about a week.

2 mugs Mung Beans, soaked in 1 mug of Water
2 Onions, finely chopped
2-3 Green *and /or* Yellow Peppers, thick slices
2 -3 Leeks, cut in inch sized chunks
1 mug Almond Milk
Juice and zest of 1 Lime *or* Lemon
6 Cardamon Pods, husks removed
1 tablespoon Madras Curry Powder
Thumb sized knob of fresh Ginger, grated
A little fresh Coriander to taste
A little fresh Leek, finely sliced for the garnish
1 teaspoon Salt
4 tablespoons Coconut *or* Sunflower Oil for frying

Lightly dry roast the cardamon seed until warm to the touch; add the oil, onion, leek & peppers and sauté for 5 minutes. Then add the mung beans with their water, the curry powder and simmer for about 20 minutes until the mung beans are soft.

Chop the coriander stems and add along with the milk, lime, ginger and salt.
Bring to the boil and simmer for a further 3 minutes.

Serve topped with the remaining coriander leaves, the fresh leek and a swirl of soya or dairy cream.

Serve as an accompaniment to a dry vegetable dish, or simply as a thick stew.

RED LENTIL DHAL
with Caremelized Carrots

2 mugs Red Lentils, washed
4 mugs Water
2 Onions, sliced into fine rings
2 Carrots, sliced in julienne pieces
1 tablespoon Sultanas, chopped
100 grams Creamed Coconut, chopped
Juice and zest of 1 Lemon
2-4 dried Chillies, chopped
1 teaspoon Nigella Seed
2 teaspoons Cumin Seed
1 teaspoon Sweet Curry Powder
1 teaspoon Turmeric Powder
1 teaspoon Salt
4 tablespoons Coconut *or* Sunflower Oil for frying

In a large pan, cook the lentils in the water on a low heat for about 15 minutes. When the lentils have softened, add the creamed coconut, lemon juice & zest, the curry powder, turmeric, salt and simmer until the coconut has melted.

Meanwhile, in a large frying pan, dry roast the whole spices until warm to the touch. Add the oil, and being careful not to burn the spices, allow to heat through for a few minutes. Add the onion, carrot and chillies, stirring gently while the vegetables slowly caramelize; this will take about 15 minutes. Add the sultanas for the last 5 minutes of the cooking time as they tend to burn very easily.

Combine all the ingredients from both pans, stir well, simmer briefly to allow the spices to infuse.

Serve as a thick soup or a protein rich sauce, with a dash of creamy yoghurt and a minute dusting of cayenne pepper.

This dhal will set if left to cool. It may then be used as a savoury spread or paté as an accompaniment to a salad. It is especially tasty with freshly chopped tomatoes and garden fresh chives.

PUY LENTIL & TOMATO DHAL

This can be used as a sauce and is especially interesting as the puy lentil keeps its shape when cooked.

2 mugs Puy Lentils soaked in 4 mugs of Water
2 Onions, finely diced
1 Celery Stick, finely diced
1 tin Tomatoes *or* **5 fresh Tomatoes, chopped**
1 large piece of fresh Ginger, chopped
Zest and juice of 1 Lemon
2 Lime Leaves
8 Cardamon Pods, husks removed
1 teaspoon Nigella Seed
1 teaspoon Brown Mustard Seed
2-4 Chillies, dried or fresh, finely diced
Small bunch of fresh Coriander, torn
1 teaspoon Salt
4 tablespoons Sunflower Oil *or* **Coconut Oil**

Dry roast the cardamon, nigella and mustard seed in a wok. Add the chillies, the sunflower or coconut oil and warm through. Add the onion & celery, and sauté until tender.

Add the lentils *(including all the liquid)*, lime leaves, lemon juice and zest. Cover and simmer for 30 minutes. As puy lentils do have the ability to keep their shape when cooked, check to see when they soften.

Chop the ginger, sprinkle with the salt and a bare squeeze of lemon juice, keep chopping and pressing with the flat of the knife until you achieve a paste; add this and the tomatoes to the cooked lentils with perhaps a dash more water.

Once the fresh ginger has been added, cook for just a few minutes longer in order to retain that sweet gingery tang.

Serve topped with finely chopped fresh tomatoes and fresh coriander plus a good twist of black pepper.
This also makes a fantastic winter soup served with chunky toasted breads.

PHOENIX KOFTA BALLS
served in a Sizzling Lime, Coconut & Cardamon Sauce

In Indian cuisine a kofta is a patty made of pulses or vegetables, usually in a small spherical shape and often served in a tangy sauce.

The Phoenix variation uses the excess courgettes we always have in our garden from June onwards.

4 mugs Red Lentils, cooked *to the consistency of solid mash*
3 Onions, sliced in ½ rings
3 small Courgettes, grated
1 mug Oat Flakes *or* **Cornflakes, lightly ground**
2 teaspoons Cumin Seed
Salt & Pepper
2 tablespoons Coconut *or* **Sunflower Oil for frying**

Put the grated courgettes into a colander with a weighted plate on top in order to squeeze out all the excess liquid.

Lightly dry roast the cumin, add the oil and onion and sauté until glassy.

Combine the red lentil dhal, onions and courgettes and season to taste. Allow the mixture to become lukewarm for easy handling.

Sprinkle the oats or cornflakes and some seasoning onto a large plate; drop a heaped tablespoon of the mixture onto the plate. Gently roll and shape the mixture into golf size balls and set aside.

Bake the koftas at oven temperature 200°C for 15 minutes until they become firm to the touch.

We serve the kofta balls double-baked, sizzling in a lime and coconut sauce, or in a rich tomato sauce. The baked or un-baked kofta balls can be chilled or frozen for later use.

LIME & COCONUT SAUCE
flavoured with Cardamon

After watching many good cooks in India, I realized that they love their rich sauces oozing with clarified butter. It was considered that a chubby hubby equals a healthy, wealthy man.
So here is a lighter sauce option:

2 teaspoons Corn *or* **Potato Flour**
1 mug Water
1 tin of Creamed Coconut
6 Garlic Cloves, diced
Juice and zest of 1 Lime
Juice of 1 Lemon
Thumb sized knob of Ginger, diced
4-6 Lime Leaves, fresh, dried or frozen
5 Cardamon Pods, husks removed
2-4 dried or fresh Chillies, diced
1 teaspoon Salt
2 tablespoons Coconut *or* **Sunflower Oil for frying**

Lightly dry roast the cardamon; add the oil, garlic and chillies and fry until the chillies turn to a deep red and the garlic is golden. Add the flour and make a roux by gently frying until it becomes a little richer in colour.

Add the water, coconut, lemon, lime, lime leaves and salt. Reduce for at least 20 minutes before adding the ginger.

This sauce should have the consistency of a thin béchamel sauce. Pour over the pre-baked kofta balls and bake until sizzling, in a medium hot oven.

A lovely crispy crust of Bombay Mix and ground cornflakes can be popped on top in the last few minutes of baking. This sauce can also be used for a simple steamed vegetable gratin and is especially good with mushrooms and potato.

Bread Reborn

It was a roasting august afternoon and I was desperately trying to dodge the sun *(heaven forbid)* in the Northern Italian town of Orta. This historic market town is set beside one of the lesser known lakes, Lago d'Orta. Adjacent to the town plaza, the lake and its island monastery, Isola San Giulio, was glistening and reflecting the steamy heat which rolled relentlessly down from the surrounding chestnut forested mountains.

Locked in the timelessness of the summer heat, along with the poignant nostalgia of childhood memories came a slight homesickness. I drifted along, through waves of solid warmth into dreamy images of endless summer holidays. The humid scent of sun on water; sweaty deckchairs, and family picnics complete with gritty rolls, home-made cake, and 'the knotted handkerchief' as the only sun deterrent.

Suddenly Siesta was over. Shop fronts began to roll up blinds, coffee machines chugged to life; pastel coloured sugary morsels were displayed invitingly along with every type of ice cream imaginable. Blood sugar low, the hunter-gatherer in me spied amongst all the finery a huge, dark, gungy slab liberally sprinkled with caster sugar.

Time and space evaporated and my very own mum's bread pudding shone out at me, shimmering like the fata morgana of a fertile oasis in a barren dessert.

My mirage was at least part reality, the part that really mattered, and I was able to purchase, for a few *(thousand)* lire, *someone else's,* 'Mama's Bread Pudding'. As I crammed my face and slurped my espresso, cultures merged and I felt blissfully nurtured, and perhaps not quite so far from home at all.

Bread pudding began its existence as an economic necessity born from the "Waste not, Want not" school of good housekeeping. In today's age it is contemporary in its philosophy; a culinary delight, with a minimal carbon footprint; adhering perfectly to the principles of recycling... with such good taste!

SWEETS & DESSERTS

BREAD PUDDING
The Phoenix Version

Soak one mug of currants generously in sherry and a dash of brandy. Take a few pieces of yesterdays bread or scones *(ours are organic wholemeal spelt)*, remove the hard crusts and add to the currants with enough grape or orange juice to cover.

Oil an oven proof dish and fill with the mixture. Then find that fruit bowl with the over-ripe bananas, and feel really good as you peel and slice them onto the mixture.

Make custard by mixing a little corn flour, brown sugar, almond milk, a drop of vanilla essence and soya cream. Pour over the pudding, sprinkle with spliced almonds, honey, a drizzle of olive oil & nutmeg.

Cover with foil and bake slowly at a moderate heat until well risen. Remove the foil and brown for the last 5 minutes. Turn off the heat, dust with caster sugar and cinnamon, and cool slowly in the oven. Serve warm or chilled with soya cream and a drizzle of maple syrup.

A creamy egg custard can replace the non dairy custard.

P.S. We find this is a fantastic way to use up pears, kiwi fruit or indeed any fruit that is over-ripe... just in case you don't have those bananas. Mmm, all very tasty!

123

DATE AND PEAR FLAN

Our desserts use a minimal amount of sugar.
In the early days this was unfashionable.
Now all kind of natural fruit sugars are
available and people seem to appreciate the
exciting tastes of quality ingredients.

4-6 Pears, peeled and sliced
1 mug Dates, chopped
2 tablespoons Date Syrup
4 tablespoons Wholemeal Ground Rice Flour
2 mugs Almond Milk
Juice and zest of 1 Lemon
Sunflower Oil

Generously oil a flan dish.
Arrange the pears and dates in the dish
and drizzle with the date syrup.

Mix the milk with the ground rice and the
juice and zest of the lemon. *Any type of
milk can be substituted for the almond milk.*
Pour over the fruit, then glaze with a little
sugar or honey.

Bake in a moderate oven at 180°C for
40 minutes until set.
The fruit will sit a little proud of the custard.

This flan can be served warm like a pudding
or if chilled, it will cut quite well into slices.

CHOCOLATE CAKE

200 grams Sweetened Chestnut Purée
If you use non-sweetened chestnut purée add 200 grams of fine organic granulated sugar.

1 mug fine Polenta Meal
1 teaspoon Baking Powder
200 grams Silken Tofu *or* **thick non-dairy Cream**
2 mugs Almond Milk
Zest of 1 Orange
Juice of 2 Oranges
200 grams 60% Dark Chocolate, chopped
½ mug Olive Oil

Lightly oil a baking dish or individual ramekins.

Place the chocolate in a bowl over a pan of simmering water and melt slowly, adding the oil towards the end.

Meanwhile cream together the rest of the ingredients and add the melted chocolate. Stir well and pour into the baking form. Bake at 200°C for 30 minutes until firm to the touch.

This cake is very romantic, cooked in little heart shaped moulds and looks naughtily delicious served with fresh cherries and a generous swirl of cream.

Crumble, Crumble on the wall, who is the tastiest of them all?

here are some desserts that require a Holy Grail quest for ingredients. This can be daunting, but a garden, a local green grocer and the larder will give you all you ever need for filling a crumble.

In northern Italy, at the back of our house in Ameno, we had a fig tree growing out of a wall. The hardest part of making a fig crumble was reaching up for the sweetest, juiciest fruits without falling into the neighbour's nettle patch.

In the South of Switzerland, when I lived in Ticino, I could stand under the tall Persimmon trees with a large sheet and a stick and catch the ripe ones as the fruits dropped. I scooped out the soft grainy flesh and made English crumbles for my friends; sometimes adding a few chopped roasted chestnuts and very pretty, small jelly-like purple grapes. Exotic maybe, however those were the fruits to hand.

Try something different; perhaps Angelica stems with rhubarb, ginger with apple, and cinnamon with raspberry.

So what does make a great crumble?
The topping has to... well... crumble and fall apart in your mouth, be a little crunchy, a little nutty, ever so slightly sweet and have a lovely grainy flavour.

Underneath it needs to be oozing with fruit; thick, juicy, and... just very, very fruity.

ROSY APPLE & ROSE PETAL CRUMBLE

A summer's day crumble, rosy apples and the petals of a sweet scented damask rose, that grows in my garden, give this an exotic and delicate flavour.

10 Rosy Apples, cored and very finely sliced
1 mug Scented Rose Petals, freshly gathered
Juice of 2 Sweet Oranges

For the Topping:
2 mugs lightly Ground Oat Flakes
1 mug Ground Almonds
¼ mug Organic Sugar
Zest of 1 Orange
¼ mug Sunflower Oil

Rub the topping ingredients together with a light and airy touch.

Arrange the apples in a flan dish, add the orange juice and scatter with the rose petals.

Sprinkle on the topping and bake in a moderate oven at 180°C for 40 minutes or until the apples are soft and ever so slightly bubbling around the edge of the dish.

RHUBARB & RASPBERRY CRUMBLE with Vanilla & Angelica

Our rhubarb causes a flurry of excitement as they are the earliest if not the loneliest fruit in the garden. Pretty, frozen raspberries come to their rescue and turn them wickedly red.

For the Filling:
A double handful of Rhubarb, chopped
2 mugs frozen or fresh Raspberries
¼ mug Palm Sugar
1 Vanilla Pod *or* **1 teaspoon Vanilla Essence**
1 fresh Angelica Stem, chopped
1 mug Water

For the Topping:
2 mugs quality Muesli
2 mugs Desiccated Coconut
½ mug Demerara Sugar
½ mug Sunflower Oil
1 teaspoon Cinnamon Powder

Cook the rhubarb, sugar and vanilla in the water for long enough to soften, pour into a flan dish with the raspberries and cool to room temperature. Meanwhile, place the dry ingredients in a bowl and rub in with a light touch; air is the secret ingredient in a good topping.

Add the angelica to the fruit and then cover with the topping. bake in a moderate oven at 180°C for 30 minutes or until the fruit begins to simmer.

127

Muesli or 'The Greater Grater'

hile working in Copenhagen I applied for a job as a cook at a Holistic Centre in Switzerland. I then set off down the long road south with not much more than my ferry fare in my pocket.

The Divine Farm was situated at the end of a forest, the last building left standing in a valley, before it was flooded to create a beautiful and ghostly lake. There was a well known sculptor living downstairs whose religious statues were eerily positioned in amongst the trees. Vigo had flowing white hair and was a spritely vegan octogenarian who only ever ate raw food.

The young people living upstairs meditated twice daily, and were very trusting when they were confronted with an 18 year old girl, claiming she could cook. There was a solid fuel cooker in the kitchen and a massive, wood fired bakers oven outside. The cupboards were brimming with whole foods. The garden in high summer was well tended and abundant. I chopped, hacked and grated my way through the herbs, salads and all the gorgeous fruits and vegetables.

Every evening the last task in the kitchen was to soak a huge bowl of oats, ground nuts, linseed and dried fruits in water and lemon juice.

Morning meditation began at sunrise. After an hour of reflection, happy & relaxed and using the highly efficient, Dr. Bircher Benner double edged grater, a mountain of apples was grated into the soaked cereals.

To this, finely chopped pears, bananas and any other seasonal fruits or berries were added. This deliciously creamy, fruity delight was then served with runny honey or thick pear syrup.

The original recipe was invented in the early 19th Century by the food reformist Dr. Bircher Benner. It was used as part of a raw food dietary treatment for the relief of many ailments. In restaurants in Switzerland Bircher Muesli can be found on the menu. It is served as a breakfast or an afternoon snack, topped generously with whipped cream.

At The Phoenix when we serve muesli in the morning, it is then that I recall the valley; the marble figures glistening in the dawn air and the warm sunlight flickering through the beech trees, bringing with it the promise of yet another beautiful day.

APRICOT & COCONUT SLICE

The secret of this dessert is to get the biscuit base crispy.
Agar-agar is a seaweed based setting agent.

2 mugs Oat Flakes
1 mug Cornflakes
½ mug Oil
¼ mug Apple Concentrate
¼ mug Honey or sweet substitute

For the Topping:
2 mugs dried Organic Apricots, soaked in
  3-4 mugs of water
Juice and zest of 1 Lime
4 Cardamon Pods, crushed
2 teaspoons Agar-agar, dissolved in ½ mug Water
Juice of 2 Oranges
100 grams Creamed Coconut, chopped

The base: Melt the honey, apple juice and oil together in a pan.
When it is just about to boil add the oats and cornflakes.
Keep stirring and heating the flakes, turning from the base of
the pan. When the mixture is hot to the touch and the oats have
become golden in colour, press the mixture into an oiled flan
dish and set aside.

The topping: Cook the apricots in their liquid, with the lime,
cardamon and orange juice; when softened add the coconut and
the liquid agar-agar. Continue to simmer carefully, adding a
little more water if necessary. This mixture will have the
consistency of runny porridge. Remove the cardamon husks
and gently pulse the mixture with a stick blender. Pour it on
top of the base and cool, slice into serving portions before it is
thoroughly chilled. Serve with kiwi slices.

129

HALVA CREAM

We have made this tangy & creamy treat for years at The Phoenix.

Halva is a sweet Mediterranean fudge, made with sesame seeds, honey and ground nuts.

200 ml Soya Cream
100 gram piece Pistachio Halva
Juice of 2 Lemons
Zest of ½ Lemon
⅓ mug Sunflower Oil
Crystallized Ginger for decoration

Put all the ingredients, apart from the ginger, into a mixer, and blend well.

Pour into delicate glass dessert dishes and refrigerate; the mixture will set after a short while.
Decorate with a slice of lemon and chopped ginger.

This dessert keeps well in the fridge covered in cling film.

ROSE & COCONUT PANACOTTA

I love panacotta, served in an espresso cup; a smooth, and very comforting end to any meal.

1 tin of quality Coconut Milk
2 tablespoons Honey
Juice of 1 Orange
1 teaspoon Corn Flour
A few drops of Rose Essence
2 teaspoons Agar-agar
¼ mug Boiling Water

Sprinkle the agar-agar on the boiling water in a small pan. Simmer until the flakes are completely dissolved.

Heat the coconut milk with the honey; combine the orange juice with the corn flour, and add to the milk along with the dissolved agar-agar, then bring to the boil.

Remove from the heat; allow to cool slightly and then add the rose essence.
Pour into small cups and set in the fridge.

Serve with a few scented rose petals dusted with a hint of icing sugar.

Summer 2013

We came to Ireland in 1992 and began, with our ever expanding family to transform a field into a garden and an old house into a home.

We started as a Hostel serving teas and scones to passing cyclists. As our garden developed I simply did what I loved doing most: dancing, cooking, dreaming and feeding everyone with scrumptiously healthy produce.

Here, at The Phoenix, I am forever learning and meeting fascinating people from all over the world. My story could lull a child to sleep or keep anyone awake, a mere drop in the vast ocean of a life. A never ending tale...

In 2011 The Phoenix was happy
to welcome John and Francis Brennan,
who filmed us for their popular TV show
'At Your Service'.
Thanks to them, the 1st edition of
The Phoenix Cook Book was launched
on National Irish Television.
It was a fantastic experience
enjoyed by all.

Autumn 1992

A Dedication to:

My children who keep me young at heart:
Amy, Alex, Christina, Sam, Kyle & Kim
My granddaughter Lily, who keeps me even younger
My husband Billy
Win & Paul
My family in England, Ireland, Switzerland, USA & Australia
My dear friends
My good neighbours & the community of Keel

Additional photography by:
Paul & Stan Arnold, Jane Brown, Simon Foster
Kees Pruijssers
Kyle Tyther, Manuel Zimmerman
Thanks to Kim Tyther for the definitive title

Inch Strand, Castlemaine Harbour, The Dingle Peninsula, September 2007